SMOKE PATROL

By the same author

SKI PATROL

HANK WINTON, SMOKECHASER

SMOKE PATROL

BY *Montgomery M. Atwater*

RANDOM HOUSE · NEW YORK

To Alice

Sixth Printing

XXXXXXXXXXXXXXXXXXXXXXXXXXXXXXXXX

ON A CERTAIN balmy evening in June, the massive headquarters of the U. S. Forest Service in Midvale, Montana, drowsed in the twilight. But like sleepless eyes two windows still glowed in different parts of the building. A passer-by would have thought that a clerk was catching up on a rush of office work. Or, perhaps, that some ranger just in from the mountains was tapping out a report with fingers more used to an axe or the reins of a horse than a typewriter.

As a matter of fact, two important conferences were being held. Oddly enough, most of the men in each group knew those at the other meeting well, but neither group was aware that the other was in the building. Yet what they discussed and decided at both conferences was to have unexpectedly dramatic effects on all their lives.

The first conference was quiet and dignified, as became a meeting of three high-ranking government officials. Any news reporter in the land would have given a month's pay to know that Regional Forester Manley and United States Senators Winton and Donahue were meeting. Any one of these men by himself was news. Together they were likely to be making history.

On the surface their chat appeared casual and friendly. But for three quarters of an hour, Senator Winton had been a silent witness to a duel.

It was no less deadly and in earnest because it was being fought with words instead of with swords. With all the skill of a practised cross-examiner, Senator Donahue was trying to goad the Regional Forester into some incautious or angry retort. With equal skill, Manley was parrying all the senator's hints, double-edged questions, and veiled insults.

It was the sort of contest Senator Winton could appreciate, and as the forester was having all the best of it so far, he saw no reason to interfere.

"The Forest Service is very glad to have you come

here to look us over," Manley was saying. "Naturally, our files are at your disposal. I'll make appointments for you with the various section chiefs and arrange any field trips you'd like to take."

In hidden admiration, Senator Winton thought, "He even makes it sound as if he meant it." He knew that the forester must want to brain the pair of them for bothering him at a time when the Forest Service was working day and night to get ready for the annual battle with its mortal enemy, forest fire.

"You arrive at a good time," continued Manley. "It's the start of the fire season, a busy period for us. You'll be able to watch the organization working at full capacity. Perhaps as a starter you'd like to look over our parachute firefighting unit."

Senator Winton did not miss the sudden gleam in Donahue's eye and he thought, "That was your first wrong move, Manley. Never offer a man like Donahue a target."

Senator Donahue said, "Ah yes, we hear some lurid tales of the—what is it you call them, smoke-hoppers? I suppose they bring the Service valuable publicity even though they're of little practical value."

Manley saw his mistake now, but it was too late to back out. So, like the good fighter he was, he attacked. "On the contrary. Air Service has been so successful that we're expanding it. We've put our finest fire leader in charge, and this year we're turning over to the smokejumpers the biggest and toughest job of fire control in the country."

"That's letting him have both barrels," cheered Senator Winton silently.

"Indeed?" Donahue's voice was slippery as silk. "I wouldn't care to comment until my son arrives later in the summer. Captain Donahue of the Air Forces, you know. I want his reaction to this idea of dropping people in parachutes helter-skelter all over the countryside. To me, frankly, it smacks of the carnival and seems a poor substitute for tried-and-true methods of firefighting that have been developed over the years."

From the way the fair skin above the tan line on Manley's forehead suddenly changed color, Hank's father knew that the forester had stood about as much as he could. To have this pompous, red-faced old politician who didn't know an azimuth from a pulaski start telling him how to fight forest fires was too much. Donahue had that effect on people. It was his chief weapon.

Smoothly Senator Winton intervened. "I understand you're graduating a class of smokejumpers toward the end of the month. We'll accept an invitation to be present. Now we've taken up enough of your time and we have a train to catch besides."

As the two senators walked down the empty corridors of the office building, Donahue said, "Winton, that's a very clever man back there, and I distrust clever men. Did you notice how he evaded all my questions? I finally got to him, though. Apparently this parachute thing is his pride and joy."

"Not surprising," retorted Senator Winton. "The smokejumpers are the greatest advance in fire control since we started protecting our forests instead of letting them go to blazes."

Donahue declaimed, "Perhaps so. But what the man is trying to do is so obvious. Organizations being investigated always want to steer the investigator onto their prize exhibit, to dazzle him with it. And I always fool them by accepting the bait. Manley and his smokejumpers forsooth! I'll take them apart like a dollar watch." It had often been said of

Donahue that he never made a statement, he always made a speech.

Senator Winton walked along a few paces in silence, considering his own peculiar situation. Up to this point it had been merely a humorous detail that Donahue didn't know he had a son who was a forester. Now it became dangerous, something that Donahue positively must not discover. For if he did the old fox would find some way to use the knowledge as a weapon.

Actually, there wasn't much risk. It had been agreed long ago between Senator Winton and a number of important Forest Service officers that Hank's career was never to be affected one way or the other by the fact that his father was a senator. Nothing there to worry about yet, Senator Winton decided. A lookout hidden in the immensity of the wilderness was unlikely to attract Donahue's attention. Thank fortune Hank wasn't a smokejumper! But it was time to make a countermove to let Donahue know where he stood.

He said, "Look, Tom, I know what you have in mind. Elections are coming up, and you need a little publicity so the folks will know you're on the job. That's all right. The Forest Service can stand a few stings, and there's nothing that makes head-lines like a good, rousing investigation. But the Forest Service is probably the finest federal organ-ization in the world. You know it as well as I do. So don't do anything destructive, Tom. Because I won't stand for it."

Senator Donahue looked a bit startled. Also a bit unhappy, for no one who had ever seen Senator Winton in action cared to collide with him. With-out any oratorical flourishes he said, "Well, that's a fair enough bargain, I guess. But I didn't know you were such an admirer of the Forest Service."

"You know now," said Hank Winton's father grimly.

For the second conference, seven lusty foresters had crammed themselves into the kind of cubby-hole assigned to rangers, who have practically no use for offices. The proceedings were very like a bat-tle royal. It was all right for the "high brass" to be dignified and go in for contests of wits where the turn of a word and the glint of an eye meant everything. But these were the fighting men of the Forest Service, the ones who made the long patrols and lonely stands against the red enemy. Separated for the eternity of a winter, they met with rib-shaking thumps on the back and bone-crushing handshakes.

Hank Winton, son of a senator, was proud to be a full-fledged member of that legion—a second-year man. As the boisterous greetings began to die down, he tasted the flavor of that word. Second-year man. To a forester, it meant something real. It meant a man who had survived the ruthless weeding-out process that every Forest Service recruit must undergo: the ordeal by toil of the dusty trails, the ordeal by loneliness of the lookout tower, the ordeal by danger of the fire line.

Even in that picked company Hank and his companion, Jim Dade, were worth a second glance. Hank was a regular giant, well over six feet tall. Above his wide square shoulders rode an unruly thatch of straw-colored hair and the friendliest pair of eyes outside the head of a Newfoundland pup. Standing still, he looked just a little awkward, as most really big men do. But at nineteen Hank had finally grown up to his hands and feet.

Black haired and black eyed, Jim Dade was a full

head shorter but every inch as broad in the shoulders. He moved with a curious sliding gait that any boxer would recognize instantly.

About them both, as about every man in the room, was an indescribable air of poise and competence that they wore like a uniform. It was the mark of a woodsman.

"All right, let's call this convention to order," said Ranger Crawford of the Three Rivers District. He spoke quietly, yet his voice cut through the din like a saw cutting green pine. He dropped his great, raw-boned length into the swivel chair behind his desk with a crash. Two brothers, Bob and Lane Corbett, perched on the ends of the desk. These famous trail-burners, one Chief of Wildlife Management and the other Game Warden, had run to earth so many fur and game poachers that the breed was almost extinct in their territory.

Their lean-hipped nephew, Brad Davis, came to squat against the wall with Hank and Jim. A Three Rivers second-year man like them, he was famous in his own right for his two-hundred mile race on skis against Emil Sicard, the king poacher of all. John Stemple, Crawford's alternate ranger and Hank's first friend in the Forest Service, completed the list. With a little tingle in all his nerves, Hank looked at the men at the desk, realizing that he was in the same room with three of the great woodsmen of their time and, what was more important, he was entitled to be there.

"Wonder what it's all about," he whispered to Jim. "Bet we're going onto the district right away."

"And just naturally skip smokechaser school," rebuked Jim. The way Hank's imagination ran off at every unusual happening always annoyed Jim Dade. Practical to the core, he didn't believe in trying to outguess the future. "More likely someone's got to take a transfer," he added cruelly.

That silenced Hank. Every Three Rivers man was in mortal dread of being transferred to some other district. Since Three Rivers was known to be the toughest fire district in the northwest with the hardest-driving fire boss, their loyalty was the ultimate tribute to Crawford.

The ranger spoke again: "As self-appointed chairman of this meeting, I will now ask the younger members to listen to a short lecture on careers in the Forest Service.

"As you know after a winter in college studying about them, forestry and the Forest Service are large and complex subjects. It's got to the point where no man can hope to master all angles. In other words, ambitious young punks like yourselves have got to specialize if you want to climb, and make up your minds early.

"I'll mention a few of the possibilities. There's wildlife management, forest engineering, timber management, grazing, recreation, public relations. Then there's fire control, without which there wouldn't be any of the others——"

"Ah-ah," interrupted Lane Corbett. "You promised, no propaganda."

"Objection sustained," said the ranger, smiling. "There's forest fire control, period. It will make a good deal of difference in your work and training, right away, if you boys can choose your fields. In fact, we ask you to choose."

Crawford stopped all at once. In the room there was dead silence. Carefully, the older men avoided the eyes of the younger while the moments dragged by. The silence became tense.

Hank felt confused. From two years of college

study, it was no news to him that there are many careers open to a forester. But it seemed to him that something more important was at stake here. He exchanged glances with Jim Dade, and Jim's almost imperceptible wink was all he needed. His doubts and bewilderment disappeared.

"You first, Hank," said Crawford. "What's it going to be?"

"Fire control," replied Hank instantly.

"That's for me too," put in Jim before he could be asked.

"What about you, Brad?"

There was an instant's hesitation, but Brad Davis answered decisively, "Guess I'll stick with wildlife."

"Glad that's over," said Crawford. "Now I can tell you the real news. You know that for several years the Forest Service has had a small parachute smokechaser outfit. Experimental. We had to see if it would work out as well as it seemed to on paper.

"It has. The smokejumpers are going to expand. And this will floor you: I've been offered the job of Chief of Air Service. I didn't think anything could make me trade the Three Rivers District for a brass hat's job. I accepted on one condition, that

I could take along the pick of my old outfit. John's coming, and Ben Gray, our dispatcher. And Hank, you and Jim, if you want to. What do you say?"

It was taciturn Jim Dade who practically shouted, "Smokejumpers. Wow!"

Hank nodded violently, but looked at the floor. It seemed to him that he couldn't glance up without meeting the eyes of Brad Davis, eyes that were sick with envy.

❦ TWO ❦

~~~~~~~~~~~~~~~~~~~~~~~~~~~~~~~~~~

THE SMOKEJUMPER school was a quadrangle of low log buildings surrounding a field of incredibly green grass. Tall firs and pines, their trunks as straight as soldiers on parade, hid the school from the outside world. Although a main transcontinental highway passed almost within hearing distance, few people outside the Forest Service even knew the school existed.

In the dustless mountain air every shadow was clean and sharp, and the sunlight was a golden haze on the bodies of a hundred men lined up in single file. One by one they walked up to a table where a doctor sat behind a heap of forms and medical instruments.

The physician didn't look much older than his

clients, but he certainly knew his business. Without being told, every anxious boy in the line coiling up to his desk recognized "Little Doc" Small, the famous parachuting doctor.

He worked fast but missed nothing. Already he had eliminated two candidates for smokejumper training. Not a word had been spoken, but every eye had seen him mark the application forms with a red pencil instead of a blue one.

Stripped to shorts and moccasins, Jim Dade stood before him, the long, smooth boxer's muscles rippling all over his body. Behind him towered Hank Winton.

"Little Doc" flipped his stethoscope onto Jim's chest and peered briefly into his eyes, ears and mouth. "How many lines of that chart can you read?" he asked Jim, pointing one shoulder at the placard on the wall behind him. There were about ten lines of jumbled letters, each succeeding line in smaller print than the one above.

"Down at the bottom it says 'American Optical Company,'" replied Jim cockily.

"What does the seventh line say?" snapped the doctor.

"L—K—T—O—F—R—B—Q. But I can't pronounce it," Jim joked.

"Humph. Ever jump before? Had any serious injuries, fractures, dislocations?"

Jim Dade, who feared no man on earth except possibly Crawford, suddenly turned white. "One jump last summer," he replied in a choking voice. "No serious injuries."

For a long moment he and the doctor stared at each other. It was the "Little Doc" who had set Jim's broken arm and leg after that one jump last summer.

"Well, move on," said Small. "Haven't got all week to inspect this beef." He picked up the blue pencil.

Hank ranged himself in front of the table, still shaking a little from sympathy for Dade. "Little Doc" slowly raised his eyes from Hank's feet to his head, as if he were counting floors in a building. "What's this?" he demanded. "You're at least fifteen pounds over the weight limit. We'd have to float you down with a circus tent."

James Crawford, now the Chief of Air Service, and John Stemple, still his assistant, had their office in one of the buildings which was smaller than the others and standing by itself. Pencil in hand, Stemple was hunched over a heap of typewritten lists laid out on a table. Crawford, never able to stay long in one place, was prowling about the room.

He looked out the window and said, "You've got to watch this, John. The 'Little Doc' is cutting your protégés down to size."

Stemple hurried to him. "You primed Doc, didn't you?" he asked anxiously. "About Jim's leg and Hank's being over the parachute weight limit?" Even at that distance, there was dejection in the slump of Hank Winton's shoulders.

"Oh sure," chuckled the Air Service Chief. "Doc is just getting in his bluff. He bucked a little about Jim with those two fractures. But we checked the x-rays down at the hospital, and he's all right. You couldn't really hurt that guy unless you used an axe."

Stemple went back to the table looking relieved. He asked, "How about sitting down long enough to O.K. these class rosters? They're complete now."

Crawford threw himself back onto a chair. "There's only one thing I want to make sure of," he mumbled, pawing the sheets together. "Yeah, I thought so." He crossed out a name on one sheet and added it to another.

Looking over his shoulder, Stemple let out a low howl of protest. "Boss, you aren't serious?"

Crawford put on what Stemple called his "ornery look," a widening of the mouth and a narrowing of the eyes that meant he was going to do something no one else would dare consider. "You mean Parker as instructor for Hank's class?"

"And Jim Dade's class," added Stemple.

"Well, what about it?" asked Crawford innocently. "We're planning on Hank and Jim for squad leaders, which means they need the best training we can give them. And if there's a better smoke-jumper around here than Lefty Parker, I haven't heard about him."

"You know what I mean," said Stemple. "Dade and Parker will tangle within fifteen minutes of the time they meet. So I suppose that's what you've got in mind. But I'm doggoned if I can understand why."

"Dade and Parker?" echoed the tall forester. "Oh no, it's Hank that will pin Lefty Parker's ears back for us and make him the best smokejumper fore-man in the outfit."

"Hank!" exploded Stemple. Then he was quiet for a full minute.

He thought back over all the time he had known and worked with Crawford, and the things the forester had done. Some of them looked odd at the time, but they always seemed to work out for the best. He thought of the last fire season, when Crawford had put Hank Winton and Jim Dade together over his own frantic protests. He remembered that the two young smokechasers had fought on sight like a couple of strange dogs. But in the end it had turned out just as Crawford predicted. A little of Jim's burning determination to succeed had entered easy-going Hank. And a little of Hank's generosity and good nature had entered Jim.

Stemple realized all at once what it was that made Crawford a peerless leader. Not his great skill and courage. Not his years of experience nor his deadly accuracy in guessing the direction a fire would take. Not his almost inhuman endurance, with which he could wear out three ordinary men one after the other. It was the single trait of knowing each man in his outfit better than the man knew himself, his strength and his weakness; of knowing to the inch and the hour how much the man could stand and where he could do his best. This was the reason that men called Crawford "slave-driver" and "man-burner," and then went out and fought for him as they would for no one else.

"Let me get this straight," said Stemple at last. "You're putting Lefty Parker in as instructor with Hank and Jim because Lefty needs his ears pinned back. I'm with you that far. Then you claim that Hank, the friendliest cuss that ever drew breath, will do the job for you, not Jim who would probably swing on a grizzly bear if the bear looked at him cross-eyed. . . . I don't get it."

Crawford's eyes sparkled. He enjoyed these mental duels with his chief assistant because Stemple had a way of going right to the center of any problem. He said, "You're on the wrong azimuth, that's all. First, Parker will never tangle with Jim because Parker will never crowd him. He knows Jim's reputation as a fighter as well as you do. Second, Parker's an expert jumper and firefighter, but he has two big failings as a leader: He has no patience with anyone who doesn't think and act as quickly as he can, and he's got just a little streak of bully in him."

Stemple waited, but Crawford said nothing more.

"I've seen you pull off some screwy deals in my time, boss," said Stemple at last. "Maybe you will this one. But if you don't, it means the ruination of three of our best men before the fire season even starts. . . . And I don't agree with any part of your argument."

"O.K." Crawford gave the window-rattling shout of laughter that meant he was completely satisfied.

It would be ten years before John Stemple looked back and suddenly realized that he himself had passed a test that day on his ability to make up his mind and stick to his opinion. Crawford was always testing his men, especially when they didn't suspect it. In the profession of forest firefighting, a man likes to be sure of the metal in his tools.

✸ THREE ✸

THE FIRST day of smokejumper school passed at a nerve-racking pace. Before Hank and Jim had time to get over the shock of their encounter with the doctor, they were signing the forms that made them official recruits of the Air Service. From there they went to the warehouse and drew a huge armful of equipment. What some of it was for Hank couldn't even imagine, though he recognized the smokejumper's armored suit and his jumping harness from photographs he had seen.

Smokechaser school had been tough last year, Hank thought. But there at least they gave you a little time to settle down and look around. Here they seemed to try to cram ninety minutes' time into every hour.

"There's Crawford written all over this setup," Jim panted in Hank's ear as they trotted across the quadrangle to find their sleeping quarters. "Just like Three Rivers District with a hot lightning storm moving in."

It was true that everything went like clockwork. There was haste but no confusion. At every stopping place a man was ready with answers and instructions. Somewhere along the line, Hank realized suddenly, the excited mob of recruits had turned into an organization. They were divided into groups, each with a guide who ran wherever they went. So they ran, too.

Hank began to take notice of his own group and its guide. There were four other recruits besides Jim Dade and Hank himself. All were strangers. Their instructor was worth a second look. He was as tall as Hank, but was about as different in every other way as a man could be. Where Hank was all of a size, like the trunk of a lodgepole pine, this man tapered sharply from wide shoulders to lean hips and legs. Thick, silky blond hair lay close to a rounded skull that was just a little too small for the rest of his body. He ran like an engine, without a wasted motion and without effort, and as he looked back over his shoulder Hank could see that his eyes were as green as emeralds.

This, although Hank didn't know it at the time, was Lefty Parker, veteran smokejumper and instructor.

At the door to one of the long log bunk houses, Parker halted. "Pick yourselves a place to flop," he told the group. "You'll be together all the way through the school, so bunk together. Dinner in fifteen minutes. Stay in the mess hall until the high brass get the pep talks out of their systems. Then meet me at the obstacle course at one-thirty. And when I say one-thirty, I mean one-thirty, not five seconds after."

"Businesslike sort of cuss, isn't he?" remarked Hank.

For the second-year men it was a matter of five minutes to collect their packsacks from the pile where the truck had dumped them and to unroll the sleeping bags already on their cots. All through the big room the same process was going on, and it was possible to pick out the trained woodsmen at that moment. The foresters were relaxing on their bunks while the tenderfeet still fussed with the straps of their bed rolls.

"Smart aleck," grunted Jim. "Somebody's liable to knock all the frosting off that cake."

"Think it over before you try," said a quiet voice. "Lefty's a hard man to handle."

Hank and Jim both rolled over to look at the speaker. Like themselves, he had settled down with the ease, neatness and lack of fuss of a woodsman. He was somewhat below the average height, but his body was very compact. He looked as solid as a stick of cordwood and up to this point had been about as talkative. On the bunk next to him was someone who looked like his twin brother. The remaining two members of their class were on the other side, next to Hank.

Hank said, "Guess we might as well all get acquainted. Looks like we'll be seeing quite a bit of each other in the next two weeks. I'm Hank Winton and this is my side-kick, Jim Dade."

"Two Baileys here," replied the stranger. "Rod and Tod. Twins, in case you haven't already guessed."

The Bailey twins, Hank thought, looked a good

deal more mature than most of the other parachute recruits. They might be as old as twenty-five. He turned over and with his eyes invited the others to introduce themselves. Hank had a natural gift for this sort of thing. He could go into a room full of strange people and a few minutes later, without any particular effort on his part, they would all be calling each other by their first names.

"Charley Bear Dance," said one of them briefly.

The name made Hank blink until he saw the tall, slim figure of the speaker, his shiny black eyes and hair, his high cheekbones and coppery skin. Charley Bear Dance was an Indian.

"Wimpfelburger, Joseph. Wimpy for short," put in the sixth member of the class. "Charley and I are Class of '51 in forestry school at the U. Our first season in the field, so I guess we're the greenhorns in the crowd. It's a cinch the rest of you guys have been around the Forest Service before." He grinned a big, shy, hopeful grin, like an awkward pup anxious to make friends but uncertain of his welcome.

Hank wondered briefly about Wimpfelburger, Joseph. Somehow he didn't look like a smoke-jumper. All the other candidates he had seen, whatever their size and shape, had looked trim and hard and active. Wimpy verged on being a fat boy.

"Guess we're all greenhorns as far as this racket's concerned," remarked Jim. "Unless you Bailey boys are jumpers."

"Well, as a matter of fact we are," came the reply. "We're squad leaders from Region 6. They don't go in for parachute firefighting the way you do in this region, but they keep a couple of squads on deck. We're up here for a refresher course. You know, new equipment, new methods. That's why I spoke up about Lefty Parker."

"You know him?" they questioned in chorus. "What's he like? Does he know his stuff? Been friends with him long?"

"Not friends, exactly," replied Bailey soberly. "Kind of hard to be friendly with that bird. As a matter of fact, I hate every inch of him. But he made the first parachute jump on a fire in history back in 1940. He's the best there is, and we're lucky to be in his class."

Further conversation was halted by the loud clanging of a tire iron outside the mess hall. Second-year man or raw recruit, every man at the smokejumper base knew what that meant and made a mad dash for the mess hall. There the hundred would-be parachutists sat down to the kind of meal only logging camp and Forest Service cooks can prepare. They were a keyed-up crowd, alternately noisy and quiet: noisy as friends separated for a winter recognized each other across the full length of the hall; quiet as strangers sized each other up out of the corners of their eyes.

At one end of the hall at a table by themselves sat the "overhead": the instructors; Air Service Chief Crawford; John Stemple, second in command; Dr. Small, and a man every forester in the northwest would recognize as Morrow, the Regional Fire Chief.

"Well, what d'you think of this crowd?" Crawford asked the "Little Doc."

"Finest physical specimens ever collected under one roof," replied the doctor. "Except for the class you graduated last week. And with one other exception."

"What's the exception, and how come?" demanded Crawford, sitting up a little straighter.

"Kid named Win—Wil—Wimpfelburger. Oh, there's nothing the matter with him. Passes every test, but he's just a shade low in co-ordination and reaction time. I was going to wash him out on general principles, but you know, I couldn't do it. If ever I saw a lad that wants to be a smokejumper, he's it. With those eyes looking at me, I just couldn't turn him down."

"You mean you're human?" Crawford poked the doctor experimentally with one finger as if he expected the sound of metal plates and wires.

"What d'you mean human?" flared Small. "You big timber beast, I'll——" He broke off suddenly, as he saw the grins. In the Forest Service the "Little Doc" was already a legend because of his temper and his irresistible determination to get to any forester who was hurt. For several minutes he went on sputtering like a lighted firecracker.

"Who's got this Wimpfelburger?" asked Crawford.

"Me," replied Parker. "I've already spotted him. I give him about two days."

"Well, give him his chance. But if he can't make

it, let's ground him before he gets hurt, not after," admonished the Air Service Chief. "I guess the boys are filled up. Let's get on with the show."

Someone banged a table knife against a glass, and instantly the clamorous mess hall was quiet. Any forester, young or old, would pause to listen to Chief Morrow. He had seen all the great fires beginning with the one in 1910. Terribly burned in 1929, his scarred face was visible proof that he knew what he was talking about.

The Regional Fire Chief began without introduction or preamble: "What I've got to say won't take long. Most of you know that aerial firefighting has been going on for around ten years now on an experimental basis. It has been successful beyond our greatest hopes. Some of you may not know that this year the smokejumpers step up into the big time.

"When this class graduates, there will be two hundred of you. Seems like a good, substantial number. But your job is complete fire protection of a million and a half acres of the most inaccessible wilderness in North America. About five times your number have been doing that job in the past.

"I can measure the size of your task in acres and

men. I can't measure the value of it. The rivers and streams, the timber, the grass, the fish, game and birds are beyond price. It's a great undertaking. I'll just wish you luck in it and turn you over to your boss, Jim Crawford, lately ranger on the Three Rivers District, the toughest fire district in the region, who is now Chief of Air Service."

Crawford took Morrow's place and for a moment towered silently over the room. "You men have been very carefully chosen," he said finally in his abrupt way. "By every means we have tried to eliminate the curiosity hounds and the glamour boys. We assume that every one of you is here on business. You'd better be. If you have any romantic notions from the movies about parachute jumping, forget them now. It takes our planes an hour on the average to deliver a smokejumper to a fire. It may take him five days to get back—*after* he puts out the fire. Doesn't allow much time for romance, does it?

"Two weeks from now you'll be making your first practice jumps, and some of you won't be here to make them. It's rough and we intend it to be. It costs a lot to train a smokejumper, so we can afford to teach only the best. Four weeks from to-day you'll graduate, and you might just as well have a jump on the real thing. The fire season's staring us in the face. So let's get started!"

✤ F O U R ✤

U S 1197691

IT WAS a sober crowd that filed out of the mess hall and then split up into groups on the way to meet the instructors. "And some of you won't be here," Crawford had said.

His words remained with them. Each man looked inward and wondered. "Wimpy" Wimpfelburger was actually trembling. He ranged up alongside Hank and Jim. "I've heard about you guys," he said. "You're the ones made that night jump last year. Is it really so tough, going out the first time?"

"Not so tough," replied Hank. "You just grit your teeth and give yourself a heave out the door."

"And the spotter always has a mallet," added Jim with a perfectly straight face.

"A mallet? What for?"

"To hammer your fingers if you freeze to the door."

"They do?" asked Wimpy in dead earnest. "That's pretty good. That way you've got to jump."

Hank and Jim looked at each other and then shrugged. "What'd you want to tell him a thing like that for?" chided Hank when Wimpy had drifted away. "He believed you."

"It made him quit worrying," retorted Jim. And then he added, "The poor sap. If he's a smoke-jumper, I'm Little Lord Fauntleroy."

At one-thirty exactly, Parker faced his class. Up to this point they had seen him mostly from the rear as he dogtrotted them from one place to another. Viewing him head-on and standing still, Hank realized that Lefty Parker was one of the handsomest men he had ever looked at. He looked like a magazine illustrator's idea of a movie star. Except for his head. Hank noticed it again, round as a cannonball and just a bit too small for the rest of him.

Almost before Parker opened his mouth to speak Hank knew there was going to be trouble. It wasn't what he said. It was the tone, a sort of sneering impatience as if he knew the boys would do everything wrong and he hated to waste time on them. Out of the corner of his eye Hank watched Jim's neck. It always turned red just before Jim reached the exploding point. With a well-timed nudge Hank could often divert his quick-tempered friend.

"I've read all your application forms," said Parker. "I know them by heart." His tone implied that it had been pretty dreary reading, too. "Two of you have been through this mill before. Don't let that give you the idea you know all about smoke-jumping. We've added a few wrinkles since you were here. Then we have a couple of second-year foresters. I suppose having chased a few smokes last summer makes you figure you're pretty tough characters and know something about physical condition. I guarantee that you haven't even suspected what physical condition is. Finally we have a couple of absolutely raw recruits. There's some hope for you. You don't have any bad habits or know-it-all ideas. We'll try to give you a new name, Charley; Charley Dance-On-Air. But I don't know; I've heard of hamburger and cheeseburger and limburger, but Wimpfelburger is a new one. I hope it isn't some new kind of boloney."

No one laughed at this joke. Even a good joke

wouldn't have been funny the way Parker said it. Hank winced for the chubby recruit. He always pitied anyone with an odd name. It never seemed to him that a person's name was anything to joke about. Catching Wimpy's eye, he winked, hoping to cheer him up, and got a sickly grin in return.

"Well, let's take the obstacle course and see how tough you guys really are," continued the instructor. "We call this layout the torture stakes." He walked over to a row of posts set firmly in the ground. The student smokejumpers had been eyeing them and wondering what they were for. At about knee height, each stake had a loop of webbing attached.

Parker stepped inside the loop, adjusted it to his legs just above the calves. Then, bending only at the knees, he let his body lean back until it was almost parallel to the earth. It didn't look particularly difficult. Hank and Jim and the other recruits followed his example.

"Arms across your chests," said Parker. "Let's see who reaches for the ground first."

Almost immediately the boys found out why they were called torture stakes. Every muscle in their bodies began to cry for mercy. Their ankles ached, their thigh muscles ached. Their stomach muscles ached. Their back and neck muscles ached. It seemed to Hank that his very insides ached, that he was slowly being pulled apart from every direction. He gritted his teeth and hung on.

Wimpy was the first to go. He didn't reach for the ground. He simply collapsed in a heap.

"One down, thirty seconds," said Parker. "Easy, isn't it?"

The seconds dragged by. Then one of the Bailey twins twisted sideways out of his loop and began to massage a cramp out of his leg. Hank could feel his own muscles stretching, or perhaps tearing, fiber by fiber. When he couldn't stand it another moment, when there were black spots in front of his eyes, he dropped his hands and eased himself to the ground. Jim was down and the other Bailey twin when he looked. Jim looked disgusted.

"One customer left," jeered Parker.

His wiry body motionless in its strained position, his copper-colored face impassive, Charley Bear Dance, the Indian, still hung on. He hung on an incredibly long time. Finally his whole body began to tremble as if he were having a spasm, and his arms dropped.

Parker didn't lower himself tenderly to the

ground as the others had done. He simply stood up straight and let the loop drop at his feet. He looked as fresh as if he had been lying on a couch.

He said, "Let's trot around a little so you won't stiffen up. Then we'll take the rest of the obstacle course."

So they trotted—around the quadrangle, up a steep logging road and back down again, around the quadrangle, up another steep logging road. . . .

"Guess it's settled now who's toughest," said Hank to Jim as they jogged along.

"Grandstand stuff," retorted Jim. "He's had a month's practice while we've been loafing."

Parker let up just in time. Charley Bear Dance was loping along easily, not even breathing through his mouth. Rod and Tod Bailey were hot and red-faced but still strong, and boxers like Jim and Hank could run ten miles without distress. But Wimpy was almost done. Drenched with sweat, gasping for air with his mouth wide-open, he had long since used up his endurance and had kept going on heart alone.

Parker halted near the torture stakes. For several minutes he let the class blow and watch a different group going through the same ordeal. It was a relief to see that the other recruits were having no better fortune.

Parker said at last, "We'll cool off by walking the rest of the obstacle course, and I'll show you some of the training gadgets. Then you're due for a little skull practise. Afterward we'll run the course, and that'll about kill the day."

Someone with a warped sense of humor had designed that obstacle course. There were hurdles, not high but set very close together. Even if you just walked through them it was hard to keep from catching your toes. There were long slippery logs studded with knots and snags of broken branches. It was worse than walking a tightrope. There were overhead bars where a man traveled hand over hand like a monkey, and brush entanglements where he squirmed through like a weasel. There were water jumps with the take-off lower than the landing place, and then there were swinging-ropes.

"This course is designed to develop endurance and agility," said Parker. "You'll spend a lot of time on it, so you might as well know why. It's tough and meant to be that way. You people hired out for a tough racket. When you hop out of a plane into the middle of the wilderness, you'll realize it. In the meantime you can take my word that only perfect physical condition will get you through."

At this point Lefty Parker seemed to be a different person. The sneer had gone out of his voice. It was as if he had been putting on an act before. Or maybe the sneer was natural and this was an act. The recruits hadn't known him long enough to be able to tell. Anyway, it was a welcome change.

"This is one of the training aids, not part of the obstacle course," continued the instructor. He had led them out onto a level platform that ended in a sheer twelve-foot drop into a sand heap. "This is the landing pit. When you come down in a parachute it's just like jumping off a twelve-foot wall. You have to learn to ease the shock with a half-roll and half-somersault, like this."

Parker took a couple of running steps and launched himself into space in such a way that he fell with body erect in the air. The moment his feet touched he curled into a ball and rolled forward over one shoulder. As a football player Hank could appreciate the way Parker had converted a solid collision into a glancing blow. But he had never seen the halfback who could do it as neatly.

Now the instructor led them out onto another platform. This one was much higher than the landing pit, at least thirty feet above ground. Facing it was a derrick built of logs, the boom towering above the platform. There was a pulley in the end of the boom with a heavy rope running through it.

Parker let them examine it for a minute or two and then asked, "Anyone want to guess? You Baileys keep quiet."

"Well, the snap in the end of that rope could hook into a parachute harness," said Wimpy eagerly. "I know, you hoist the boys from the ground up to this platform."

"You're warm, Cheeseburger," replied Parker. "But you've got it backwards. When you leave your plane, you fall free for about twenty feet. Then your parachute opens. It's quite a jolt. In fact until you get used to it, it feels as if your spine were coming out through the top of your head. You'll get used to it on this jump tower. By changing the length of the rope we can give you falls of any depth.

At the same time you'll learn airmanship, to jump clean and straight. In fact a lot of gents make up their minds right here that they don't really want to be smokejumpers." With these last words, Parker stared straight at Wimpy, whose eyes were roving from the dangling rope to the chasm beneath and whose face had turned the color of putty.

The instructor continued, "Got to hurry along now. Over there is the plane 'mock-up,' just a rough copy of a plane fuselage . . . It's for teaching you how to get out of the ship. It does take practice even to go through a door when there's nothing outside the door but a few thousand feet of air. That cable strung between two poles is where you work on let-down procedure. So you won't beat your brains out wondering what that is, Limburger, let-down procedure is what you do when you make a parachute landing in the top of a tree."

✲ FIVE ✲

SUPPER in the smokejumper mess hall that first night was a complete contrast to the noon meal. There wasn't a sound except the occasional clink of fork or knife. The recruits were too tired to talk. Wimpy had been so exhausted that he refused to get off his bunk when the tire iron had clanged its summons. Between them Hank and Jim cajoled their classmate into going along. Once at the table, Wimpy revived and ate as ravenously as the others did. But after supper the last smokejumper was in bed and asleep while it was still daylight.

For a week they staggered through the merciless routine of obstacle course, landing pit, jump tower, plane mock-up and let-down apparatus plus the most fiendish set of calisthenics ever devised. The calisthenics began with twenty push-ups done not on flat hands but the fingertips. Among the hours of physical conditioning came all too short periods of classroom instruction, during which they could actually sit down.

A few empty beds appeared in the bunk houses, gaps that no one ever mentioned but everyone saw and thought about. But by the end of that first week, the amazing powers of youth and health began to show. The recruits could hang at the torture stakes for minutes at a time, bouncing up and down and talking to each other. Now a simple run and leap into the landing pit was too easy. The idea was to make a broad jump out of it. Dr. Small had to put a stop to this game when the contestants began jumping all the way over the sand bed and landing on hard ground. Three sprained ankles in one day brought him out sputtering with rage.

At the jump tower the rope was at its maximum length. Many a bone-wrenching jar had taught the recruits to jump straight and clean and to adjust the complicated harnesses to a hair's breadth, so that the shock was evenly distributed. Their bitten tongues and lips and the unexpected jerks they felt when the derrick man changed the length of the rope taught them to keep their mouths closed and their eyes open.

All the recruits liked the tower. It was exciting. For one thing, they worked on the tower in the full panoply of the smokejumper, except for the parachute. They liked the business of helping each other into their armored jump suits and adjusting the harnesses. Naturally this called for a good deal of horseplay and joking back and forth. The instructors and the few professionals like the Bailey twins pretended to be very bored by the roughhousing. But they fooled no one. If it hadn't been a question of their dignity, they'd have joined in and everybody knew it.

Then there was the routine of marching out to the edge of the platform, hooking the risers of the parachute harness to the rope, jerking them to make sure the connection was secure, waiting for the signal to jump. Finally, then, the tap on the shoulder and the leap into space.

It doesn't take very long to fall twenty feet. But

during that breathless moment when a man feels the tremendous force of gravity plucking him earthward at an ever-increasing speed, a great many pictures race through his mind. He forgets that this is only a platform built of logs, that he is attached to a rope strong enough to check the fall of a horse, that there is a safety net under him just in case something does go wrong. What he sees is a plane floating over a limitless jumble of mountain, canyon cliff and forest. He sees himself poised in the windy door, not thirty feet up but three thousand. Eyes fixed on the telltale plume of smoke that is his goal, he makes the plunge into empty space. And when the rope checks him with its familiar jerk, he hears not the clashing of the pulleys but the thunder of his opening parachute.

The recruits heartily despised two of their training aids. One was the plane mock-up. That plank and scrap-iron monstrosity, without wings, without grace, without the power of motion, looked just enough like an airship to be an insult. Day after day the recruits filed in through the door, ranged themselves along the walls, moved in order back to the door, went through the routine of hooking up, testing, getting ready to jump and jumping—onto the ground two feet below.

They practised this simple and tiresome process day after day and hour after hour until the mere sight of the mock-up made them ill. They also learned to empty a plane in about one-tenth the time it had taken them at first.

The other pet hate of the recruits was the let-down apparatus. Here too they practised in full equipment. But there was nothing about this part of the training to stir the imagination. The let-down apparatus was a cable strung high overhead between two tall poles. A number of pulleys were fastened to the cable with a rope running through each pulley.

From daylight to dark there were always smoke-jumpers dangling under the cable like laundry hung out to dry. The routine was quite simple. They hung there in their harnesses, unable to touch anything, just as they would if they made a parachute landing in a tree. Those twenty, thirty, perhaps a hundred feet to the ground could be just as tough a problem as the two or three thousand they would already have dropped. They could be even tougher. Maybe the jumper would be dizzy and hurt from being thrown against the tree by a gust of wind, or tangled in his rigging. In any case, a smokejumper is of no use to anyone until his feet are on the ground.

Over and over the instructors dinned this fact into the ears of the recruits. Over and over the recruits practised. You reached for the end of your let-down rope in the pocket on the leg of your jump suit. In and out you wove it through your harness according to a certain pattern. You hooked it into the ring overhead where the risers from your harness met the shroud lines of your parachute. You dropped the coil of let-down rope to the ground. Then you struck the quick-release buckle of your harness, and the whole complicated tangle of rigging fell apart and left you free to slide down the rope to earth.

Very simple, this let-down procedure. But it could also be tricky, as the recruits discovered. One little mistake in weaving that rope through the harness, and your rigging didn't come apart. Instead it turned into a snarl of straps and cords and buckles that held you like a fly in a spider web; upside down, as likely as not.

On the let-down apparatus, this merely meant

being lowered ignominiously to the ground with the catcalls of your friends and the disgusted comments of your instructor burning your ears. On a fire jump in the middle of thousands of square miles of wilderness it would probably mean a job for Doc Small. And, as the instructors were fond of remarking, an injured smokejumper puts out no forest fires.

So the young parachutists worked at let-down procedure until they could make that important little rope pattern one hundred times out of a hundred with both hands, with either hand, with eyes closed, even, to hear them tell it, in their sleep.

Oddly enough this was the one part of the training in which Wimpy excelled. Even Parker seemed glad to find him excelling in something. After the first inevitable mistake in lacing the rope through his harness, Wimpy never made another. Day after day, in competition against his mates or against other classes, he was always the first to hit the ground. The secret, Hank eventually decided, was that all Wimpy's skill was concentrated in his hands.

It wasn't that Wimpy was actually clumsy or slow in thinking. In spite of his chubby figure, he was tough and strong. He caught a new idea as quickly as anyone else, and he had enough determination for two smokejumpers. It was just that he lacked that razor-edged coordination of eye, nerve and muscle that was practically the badge of a parachutist. They all had it, tall or short, lean or stocky, professionals like the twins or raw recruits like Charley Bear Dance. It was in the way they moved, even in the way they sat, a cat-like quality of speed and precision. The ones who didn't have it had long since disappeared from the school—except Wimpy.

It had been a terrific job to get him this far. Hank took care of him as a matter of course. It was as natural for the big second-year man to help someone who needed help as it was for him to breathe. After a good deal of grumbling that Hank was merely wasting time and getting himself into trouble besides, even Jim took a hand. But he did it for Hank, not for Wimpy.

Everything that black-haired forester possessed he had fought for and won with his own hands and brain. "Each man for himself" was Jim's creed. But like all utterly self-reliant people, he had to have one anchor outside himself that he believed in and trusted without even realizing it. For Jim Dade that anchor was Hank Winton, the man he had quarreled with and envied and despised throughout one fire season; the man who had finally won his friendship.

There was nothing complicated about the world to Jim Dade. It was all black or all white. So if Hank wanted to hurt his chances in the Forest Service by trying to hold up a dub, there was nothing for Jim to do but pitch in alongside him.

As a matter of fact, the whole class pitched in. The Bailey twins taught Wimpy little short cuts and tricks of the trade they had learned from hard experience. Charley Bear Dance, who spoke barely ten words a day, always had a question to ask when Parker was about to go into one of his tirades on the general uselessness of Limburger or Hamburger or whatever name he had thought up for that day. They all tried to catch Wimpy's mistakes before he made them or cover up for him after he made them.

Whether they wanted to help Wimpy or thwart Parker it would have been hard for any of them to say. Probably it was about half and half. They all liked Wimpy. He was so willing, so eager to please and so determined to make the grade. Parker was a mystery to them. They respected him as an ace instructor who knew his subject to the last detail. The contemptuous, impatient way he treated them all wouldn't have mattered. It got results, and they were prepared to accept it as his method of turning them into smokejumpers in the shortest possible time. And there were those unexpected moments when Parker forgot to sneer. It was Hank who discovered that if they could get him started on the early days of smokejumping he was an entirely different person. But the way he persecuted Wimpy was unbearable. He seemed to have a cold-blooded determination to break the boy. So, without a word spoken, they turned against the instructor and, if they had only known it, made Parker as baffled and uneasy as they were.

Hank thought he had the problem solved one day. After a particularly savage and unwarranted attack on Wimpy, Hank went to Crawford. In secret, of course. He knew Jim would have disapproved violently.

He asked Crawford to put Wimpy in a different class.

The forester's reaction surprised him. Crawford looked at him through half-closed eyes in the off-hand way he had that meant he was tuned up like a high-frequency radio.

"Whose idea was this?" he asked. "Yours or Wimpfelburger's?"

"Oh, mine," admitted Hank at once. "Wimpy wouldn't say anything. But for some reason Parker's got a peeve on him. I suppose it's because Wimpy's a little slower on the uptake than the rest of the gang and Parker doesn't want to bother with him. So he's trying to make Wimpy quit."

This was a much shrewder observation than Hank realized, and it made Crawford close his eyes completely.

"Don't think much of Parker, do you?" remarked the Air Service Chief.

"He's a champ instructor," replied Hank. "But I sure don't like him. If that's what you mean. Nobody does."

After a moment of silence Crawford said, "I'm going to tell you a little story, Hank. When I got my first appointment as an alternate, they put me out with an old-time ranger, one of the originals. He didn't have a college degree in forestry, he never went to guard school or got any of the help and training you young punks get nowadays. But believe me, he was a forester. He was also the most cantankerous, opinionated, unreasonable old wood tick that ever drew breath. The first month I was with him I thought I'd quit the Forest Service. The second month I thought I'd end up by killing him. I didn't do either, fortunately, and I learned more about fighting forest fires from the ornery old devil than I've ever learned since.

"The point is that if you have to work with a man it's nice if you like him. But it absolutely is not necessary. If anybody knows that, you ought to."

This was a clear reference to Hank's troubles with Jim Dade the summer before. Hank felt his ears grow hot with embarrassment and wished he had thought over his idea more carefully before acting on it. When he looked up, Crawford was grinning at him.

"Don't take it so hard," said the forester. "I know your buddy's having a bad time. But this isn't a game, and he'll just have to tough it out . . . Where's your father these days, Hank? Thought he'd be taking the kinks out of his fishing tackle before now. In fact, I have some water all picked out for him."

Hank grinned back in relief. When you made a mistake with Crawford, you were told off, but that was the end of it. He said, "Oh, Dad's snooping around out here someplace. Jim and I came out on the same train with him. But he was trailing with another big shot, so officially we were strangers."

Crawford chuckled. He knew about this arrangement between the senator and his son. Unless warned in advance, no one ever suspected the small, trim senator of being the father of a giant like Hank. It was a highly efficient arrangement, for Hank had an almost terrifying ability to collect information. It seemed as if people just couldn't help talking to him.

"Fishing pal of his?" asked Crawford.

"Senator Donahue?" Hank laughed. "Well, hardly. In a polite way, and all according to the rules of order, they've been cutting each other's throats for years. No, they're probably on a Congressional investigation. Very top secret. Dad wouldn't tell me a thing about it."

"Probably because it's the Forest Service they're investigating," suggested Crawford.

"The Forest Service!" cried Hank in horrified tones. "Why would they want to do a thing like that?"

"Well, why not? You may not have discovered it yet, but the Forest Service has many enemies. It's big and powerful, so it's bound to have them."

Hank could only shake his head in unbelief.

✤ S I X ✤

IT WOULD have amazed any of the smoke-jumper recruits to know how carefully they were being watched. There were no examinations or grades. True, Crawford and Stemple and the "Little Doc" were always wandering around the training area, asking a few questions and then going on, but it seemed entirely casual.

Yet they couldn't help noticing and being curious one evening near the end of the second week of training. The complete "overhead" of the parachute school—the Air Service Chief, Stemple, Doctor Small and all the instructors—disappeared into Crawford's office.

Their curiosity would have been feverish if they had known that the instructors were reporting on the recruits, class by class and man by man. At the moment it was Parker's turn. Among people who were his equals in experience and ability, his pupils wouldn't have recognized their "Little Caesar." He spoke quietly and without any sneer.

"Guess I don't need to say much about the Bailey twins," he began. "They've been through the mill before and they'll take good care of things down California way. Charley Bear Dance, new man. You never know for sure, of course, until they make that first jump, but if he isn't a natural, I never saw one. Dade and Winton, couple of second-year men; squad leader material as soon as they've had a little actual experience. Cheese—I mean Wimpfelburger——" The instructor hesitated.

"Well, what about Wimpfelburger?" asked Crawford.

"I've tried every way to break that guy," said Parker flatly. "He'll never make a smokejumper, so it looked like the best thing to get it over with quick."

"Nothing wrong with his let-down technique," remarked Stemple.

Crawford added, "If he can't make the grade, how come he's got this far?"

"He wouldn't have except that Winton's propping him up. All of them for that matter, but mostly Winton. I don't know why." Parker sounded angry and puzzled. He looked up just in time to intercept a meaning glance that Crawford shot at Stemple.

"Are you recommending that we drop Wimpfelburger?" asked the Air Service Chief.

Parker shook his head. "Nope. He's entitled to his chance now. But I don't think he'll ever jump."

"O.K. That's how it'll be, then. Doc, we're ready to hear from you. What kind of shape's the outfit in?"

"Never saw a bunch of men train any prettier," snapped the doctor. "But there's your best answer."

He pointed with his chin out the office window, and all eyes followed his motion. Outside lay the emerald expanse of the quadrangle. For a long time it had been empty except for classes going from one training station to another, and had been completely deserted after working hours. Not now. Several noisy softball games were in progress. A clanging sounded from the horseshoe-pitching stakes. The instructors could see any strenuous activity from Indian wrestling to pole-vaulting wherever they might look.

"How hard can a bunch of men get?" demanded the "Little Doc" dramatically. "When eight hours of what we dish up can't send them to bed, they're in shape."

Crawford nodded. "We'll go ahead then and schedule the first practice jump. I'm glad to see things coming along so well—for a special reason. The grapevine has it that some big shots from Washington are going to be around for the graduation show."

"In that case I suppose you'll cancel the mass jump in favor of something more foolproof," said Parker.

"Not at all," retorted the Chief of Air Service. "It means a little extra wear and tear on you instructors. But I'm confident you can put the show across."

Crawford managed to put something special into these left-handed words of praise without moving in his chair or raising his voice. How he did it is impossible to describe, but each instructor left the office feeling that he had received a personal pat on the back. They all needed one. Though it would never have occurred to the recruits, the training grind was hard on the instructors too. This was their second round of taking a group of raw, awkward volunteers and turning them into skilled fighting machines. But the best medicine for their strained nerves was the fact that Crawford would stake his reputation on them. For a leader like that, men do the impossible.

If the members of Parker's class could have heard what their instructor had just said about them, they would have gaped with astonishment. From the Bailey twins, who had already proved their ability, to the ever-hopeful Wimpy, each one of his student parachutists looked on himself as the instructor's pet hate. This belief had made the five recruits draw much closer together than the boys in other classes. Parker's students had a tendency to herd by themselves at all times.

"Well, I see the brass are calling it a day," remarked Hank. Lounging on the grass, he looked relaxed and half asleep. But he had more than a touch of Crawford's awareness of everything that went on around him. "Wonder what devilment they've cooked up now?"

"Wonder who got the axe?" asked Jim, going as always direct to the point.

Charley Bear Dance, cross-legged and motionless as a statue, made one of his rare contributions to their talk. "I figure things will ease up after the first jump. You'll either be in or out."

"But when's that going to be?" groaned Hank. "There's such a thing as overtraining and going stale."

They batted this conversational ball around the circle for several minutes until Hank spotted knowing grins on the faces of the Bailey twins.

"All right," he said. "What are you two jokers looking so wise about?"

"Don't forget we've been through this before," replied Rod—or Tod. No one could tell them apart, so no one tried any more. "You'll jump, and plenty soon enough. Want to know the sure sign?"

"You bet. Spill it," came the chorus.

"When we take our trip through the chute loft."

"Oh-oh," said Hank. "I happened to take a squint at the bulletin board on the way over here, and you know what it says? 'All classes tour parachute loft tomorrow.' "

In the excitement over that bit of news not even Hank noticed that Wimpy had turned as white as a parachute.

✿ SEVEN ✿

THAT MORNING began like any other at the smokejumper school, with the familiar calisthenics. The session would have put any ordinary human being in bed for the rest of the day. But the young smokejumpers weren't ordinary human beings any more. They were trained to the absolute peak of physical condition. They raced through the routine and then looked expectantly at their instructors. For they weren't blind. That long line of Forest Service trucks parked around the quadrangle wasn't there by accident. And those tight canvas bundles heaped in one of the trucks weren't cushions, either. They were parachutes. And this was a day anticipated and dreaded—the day of the first parachute jump.

Being only human, the instructors kept up the

suspense as long as they could. Then the announcement, "Get full jumping equipment and load into those trucks," sent the recruits running for the warehouse. The instructors followed at a more leisurely gait, for they were going to jump too. But try as they would, they couldn't keep a sparkle out of their eyes or a certain tension out of their voices. Stepping out an open door into a mile or so of empty air is an adventure that never grows monotonous, the first time or the hundredth.

Packed into the trucks like sardines, the recruits jounced the few miles to the Forest Service airfield. It was the first time they had been outside the training camp for two weeks. With some surprise they noted that the ordinary world was still there, exactly as they had left it. Cars whizzed back and forth on the highway, farmers tilled their fields, housewives hung out the wash, trains rumbled past and no one seemed a bit excited over the fact that a hundred young Americans were about to make the first parachute leaps of their lives.

The same casual air pervaded the flying field. A fat-bodied transport plane with Forest Service markings squatted at one end of the field. To one side the horn of a loudspeaker pointed its iron throat at the sky. Otherwise there seemed to be no preparations whatever for this climactic moment. The taut nerves of the recruits relaxed. After all, it was just another day's work.

There was a good deal of unnecessary chatter as the smokejumpers climbed out of the trucks and helped each other into their bulky jump suits. But it had lost the high-pitched note of hysteria. While the laggards were still fussing with the buckles of their harness, the plane waddled out into the center of the field. It swallowed fifteen armored, helmeted figures, the instructors, and was in the air almost before the door slammed shut. Any second-year man from a back country ranger district could recognize that technique, the mark of a Forest Service bush pilot who wouldn't have known what to do with a mile-long runway if he'd had one.

"Nice to see we get the best," muttered Jim Dade.

"What d'you mean?" asked Hank.

"Bob Johnson's flying us," came the reply. With respect unusual for Jim, he spoke the name of the greatest bush pilot of them all.

As the plane made its wide turn and came back toward the field, John Stemple's voice boomed from the loudspeaker: "The air is flat calm, so the instructors are going to save us a little time and gas and will jump without sending down a pilot chute. Watch their chute handling. You'll never see any better."

With fascinated attention, the recruits watched the approach of the plane. They saw the square black opening in its side, the first helmeted figure poised on the step.

Every detail was clear as if seen through a telescope in slow motion. They saw the thrust of his arms as he launched himself, the static cord looping out behind him. They saw his parachute pack burst, spouting yard after yard of nylon. Then, too quick for the eye to follow, the canopy opened with a report like a rifle shot. The plummeting figure checked and hung motionless under its dome of white.

Fifteen times this was repeated, faster than a man could count. The plane droned away, leaving them strung as evenly as beads on a cord.

Now they broke formation as each jumper steered

for a landing place. "We don't expect you to unload quite that fast," remarked the loudspeaker to the watching boys. "The thing we want you to watch is the chute handling. You've been told that the Forest Service parachute is maneuverable. Now see the demonstration." The horn turned skyward and bellowed, "All jumpers turn round to the right."

Obediently each dangling figure executed a slow right whirl.

"Now steer to the right. Now steer to the left."

In this queer aerial dance, the jumpers dropped lower and lower. "O.K., you're on your own," came the final command. By now they were close enough so that it could be seen how each jumper pulled his guide lines to open and close the steering slots in the parachute. The watchers even fancied that they could recognize individuals.

Whether he did it deliberately or not, his pupils never knew, but Parker came to earth directly in front of his class, not over twenty feet away. He performed the unusual feat of landing without any roll and somersault to break the shock. He just landed, compressed himself like a spring and then shot up again to his full height. For thirty interminable seconds he looked at them while his hands drew on the shroud lines of his chute until he had its gleaming folds in his arms. In that moment his pupils vowed silently they would forgive him every sneer, every tongue-lashing, every weary hour he had driven them, if only they could handle a parachute like that.

At last he said harshly, "This is where we separate the men from the boys. When you're up there yourselves, remember these two things: Jump clean, and as soon as your chute opens, get hold of those guide lines.

"There will be four classes in each plane load. One class jumps on each run over the field; your class jumps last of the four in your plane. You'll jump in the following order: One, Rod Bailey; two, Tod Bailey; three, Charley Bear Dance; four, Jim Dadc; five, Joseph Wimpfelburger; six, Hank Winton.

"Remember your number so when Stemple talks you down over the loudspeaker you'll know which one he means. And one more thing. You may have heard that if you don't feel just right you can skip the first pass and ride around for a second try. Not in my class you can't. Jump the first time or don't jump at all."

"Let's go. We're on deck."

Now that he was in the plane and actually about to make his first practice jump, Hank found that he couldn't get excited about it any more. To his own surprise, he felt angry, not at anybody or anything; just an all-around irritability and a desire to get the jump over with. A glance at his companions gave him no clue to their emotions or thoughts. Some had already put on their steel-meshed helmets and were faceless. The others might as well have been, for all Hank could tell from them.

The steady roar of the airplane engines made conversation impossible. Hank felt that he had to exchange ideas with someone. He nudged Jim and got a sullen glare from his friend. He turned to Wimpy on the other side and thought he had never seen such a look on a human face. Wimpy's eyes were wide open and staring; his mouth worked as if he were trying to chew something, and his face was shiny with sweat.

Hank winked and grinned at him. For a second Wimpy stared right through him. Then his eyes focussed and he shouted something. To Hank it sounded as if he said, "I can't, I can't." But that couldn't be right, so Hank shook his head and pointed to his ears.

At this moment the class nearest the door got up and began to scramble awkwardly into jump position. They hooked their static cords into the bar in the roof of the cabin, and their instructor took his place at the spotter's window signaling course changes to the pilot; their lead-off man edged out onto the step, half in, half out of the doorway.

Now the spotter chopped his hand toward the floor, and the engine noise faded. He touched the lead-off man on the shoulder, and as if released by a spring, that man plunged into space. In a clumsy rush, the others followed him. It wasn't like the smooth performances on the mock-up. But then neither was this like jumping out onto the ground. With a satisfied grin, the instructor reeled in the flapping static cords while the reports of the opening parachutes thudded against the metal hide of the plane.

The second class jumped, again without a hitch. Looking down as they passed over the field, Hank could see the parachutes of the first group crumpled on the ground.

The third class jumped. In this group the last man checked as he reached the door. It was almost as if he had run into something solid. Then he backed up a pace and plunged through head first and sprawling. The instructor looked anxiously out the door after him and then smiled and shook his head. With gestures he described the bruises a man would get for jumping like that.

And now the plane was empty except for the figure of Parker at the spotter's post and the six outlandish figures of the twins and Charley and Jim and Hank and Wimpy. The ship made its long, slow turn. It leveled off and bored in straight over the field. With professional skill the twins snapped their static cords to the bar. The others imitated them. Now they were lined up behind Rod and waiting for the signal.

Parker gave that downward chop and the tap on the shoulder. Rod was away. His brother followed smoothly. Charley Bear Dance let out a triumphant screech as he cleared the door. Jim Dade jumped in grim silence.

Wimpy was next, and when he came level with

the opening he halted as if his feet had suddenly stuck to the floor. Hank, unable to check his own rush in time, ran into him. The strange tableau held for a second. Then Parker shouldered Wimpy to one side and waved Hank on.

Hank tensed himself and in the same moment halted again. Without conscious thought, without knowing how he made the decision, he knew that he could not leave Wimpy alone in the plane with Parker. He took off his helmet, looked at the instructor and made a circling motion with his hand. He saw the pilot, who was watching over one shoulder, shrug, then nod and turn back to his controls. The expression on Parker's face was almost indescribable, compounded of amazement, disgust and pure rage.

Hank sat down. Right through the heavy jump suit he could feel the shuddering of the figure beside him. He put his mouth to Wimpy's ear and shouted, "It's all right, Wimp. Lots of guys pass up the first run. I'll go ahead this time. You hang onto my belt and close your eyes. Got it?"

Wimpy turned an agonized face to him for a moment and nodded.

In this manner Joseph Wimpfelburger, recruit

smokejumper, made his first leap. Blindly he was dragged by Hank Winton into space. Like a sack he hung in his harness after his parachute opened, making no attempt to maneuver for a landing. Hank hovered around him anxiously, yelling at him to snap out of it and take hold of his guide lines. Stemple finally ordered him away over the loud-speaker, warning him to pay attention to his own landing.

Without ever making a motion after he left the plane, Wimpy thudded to earth. Hank landed close by, but the first man to reach the unconscious body was the "Little Doc," who pounced on Wimpy like a ferret and had him out of his jumpsuit in three slashes of his knife.

Crawford and Stemple joined him in a moment and the smokejumpers made a circle of staring eyes. For a while there was complete silence as the doctor worked with deft hands. At last he drew back and looked at Crawford.

"What is it, Doc?" asked the Air Service Chief.

"Believe it or not," said the "Little Doc." "He's fainted."

✤ EIGHT ✤

THERE was little activity on the quadrangle that evening. The regular training grind might not have exhausted the smokejumpers, but the events of this day had. Only one half-hearted softball game was going on. The horseshoes clanked at long intervals. Parker's students were by themselves as usual, but now they were very obviously oustide the common circle. Two jump refusals, and both in the same class; the only refusals of the day. The rumor was spreading rapidly that the axe had already fallen on Hank and Wimpy.

Realizing at last what he had done, Hank felt curiously unmoved. It still seemed to him that he couldn't have deserted Wimpy. Unable to talk him out of this notion, Jim had turned away in disgust.

No one was acting in a normal manner. For Jim next pounced on the despairing Wimpy and inveigled him into a boxing match. But it was like no contest Jim Dade had ever engineered before. With unbelief, Hank saw that Jim and Wimpy were merely batting at each other. Jim was letting the disgraced smokejumper hit him. It was incredible, but it was the only tonic that could have done Wimpy any good at the moment. The idea that he could actually lay a glove on Jim Dade, known to be a professional and deadly fighter, was putting a spark back into his lifeless eyes.

Into this scene strolled Lefty Parker. In the mildest tone he had ever used to Wimpy, he said, "How about sparring a round or two with me?"

Sullenly Jim handed over his gloves and backed away. Wimpy looked uneasy and puzzled. Hope put the thought into his head: "Could this be forgiveness?"

"Why sure. Glad to," said Wimpy.

The two squared away and Wimpy pawed experimentally at the instructor. Then Parker stepped in and with all his power, smashed him in the face.

Blood spouted from Wimpy's nose and welled

from split lips. His knees buckled. But he did not fall. In the next few moments, he proved several things, that he was tough and strong—and that he had courage. Unable to raise his hands, with a grin that was the more terrible because it had no meaning, he marched into the fury of Parker's fists.

The unequal contest lasted only a few seconds, just long enough for Hank to jump up and cross ten feet of grass. Jim tried to hold him back with a "Keep out of this, you fool." But Hank shook him off. He didn't even hear the advice Jim called after him, "Well, then watch that shift. Remember he's a southpaw." Looking awkward as a two-year-old colt, all knobby joints and big bones, he shuffled out into the arena. He got between Parker and Wimpy and it seemed as if by accident that Parker's Sunday punch glanced off Hank's shoulder.

"How about a round with me, Lefty?" he asked.

Parker drew back, glaring out of eyes wild with rage. "Never say you didn't ask for it, big boy," gritted the instructor.

Like iron particles attracted by a magnet, the smokejumpers formed a circle. And others had seen what was going on. In Crawford's office, John Stemple turned from the window with worried eyes. "You were right," he said. "Hank and Lefty Parker are fighting. I'll go stop it."

"Oh no you don't," retorted Crawford, collaring him with one huge paw. "This is the pay-off. This is where I get a first-class smokejumper fore-man or——"

"Or nothing," said Stemple gloomily. "Had you considered that?"

"Or nothing," Crawford agreed grimly. "That chance has to be taken. It's all up to Hank now."

"I won't have it," protested Stemple. "Does poor Hank have to get beaten up for your blasted experiment?"

"Poor Hank!" Crawford barked out a laugh. "And him trained by Jim Dade? You mean poor Parker."

The instructor waded into Hank as he had into Wimpy, battering at him savagely with both fists. But the results were quite different. Presently Parker realized that his wild blows were landing on nothing. Instead of driving Hank back step by step, he was backing up himself under a series of light taps on his jaw. At least they felt light; yet the shock ran all the way to his heels.

Parker broke away. The wild light in his eyes vanished and was replaced by fierce pleasure. This was going to be a real battle, not a slaughter, and he welcomed it. He shook his head, which momentarily was full of cobwebs, and then came in again. This time he attacked with a flurry of short, powerful roundhouse punches.

Delivered by a man as fast and as strong as Lefty Parker, they would have won any ordinary fight very quickly. In fact, most of the spectators thought Hank was taking a terrific beating. It looked as if he were being overwhelmed. Only a trained eye like Jim Dade's could see what was actually going on. Hank moved his head a fraction of an inch and rolled Parker's punches over his shoulders. He let them slide off his forearms, he caught them in his gloves. And all the time his left kept driving in and out, in and out, too fast for the eye to follow. But Parker's head, bobbing back and forth like an apple on a string, told the tale to Jim.

For a second time Parker broke away. His breath

was rattling a little in his throat, but he was not really tired or hurt. It was just that his eyes wouldn't focus, and Hank appeared to him as a blur. Not yet had it occurred to the instructor that he was being cut to pieces as methodically as a log in a sawmill.

Hank sparred with him deliberately while he recovered. For one of the few times in his life Hank was really angry and he intended Parker to taste every bitter drop of defeat.

It took something special to make Hank Winton that angry. A man letting a forest fire get away for private gain, for instance, or beating up a harmless, eager beaver like Joseph Wimpfelburger. Realizing what was going to happen, Jim muttered, "I ought to go get Doc." But he could not bring himself to leave.

As Parker's eyes and mind cleared, he really looked at Hank for the first time since the beginning of the fight. What he saw was not very encouraging: two eyes cold as glacier ice peering at him over the point of Hank's shoulder. Hank's jaw was tucked in behind that shoulder, his upper arms lay close to his sides, protecting his ribs, his forearms blocked the way to his midriff, and always the two bludgeons of his fists wove in and out, agile as snakes. To the baffled instructor he presented no vulnerable target whatever.

When he came in again, Parker was more cautious. He feinted, trying to force some opening in that barricade of bone and muscle. Hank lowered his guard temptingly and then moved inside Parker's overhand smash at his face, the same punch that had wrecked Wimpy. Almost chest to chest with the instructor, he battered the soft spots just at the edge of the ribs.

To Parker it felt as if knives were being driven into him. Three times he tried his feint-and-punch attack. Three times the agony of Hank's counter blows made him retreat. And then Lefty Parker knew that he was licked.

At this point the ordinary bully would have looked for some way to call off the fight and save his face. Not Parker. Whatever else he might be, he was no coward. Grimly he came on for the last time and with his last trick. He had been fighting like all untrained fighters, facing his opponent almost square and flat-footed, swinging with both hands. Suddenly now he took the boxer's one-foot-forward stance and launched a desperate one-two punch.

Hank had never before fought a left-handed opponent, and Parker's southpaw attack caught him off balance, as many an older boxer has been caught. He shrugged off the lead punch, but the follow-up went home.

It stung, and Hank reacted like a tiger poked with a stick. He forgot all about his plan to cut Parker to pieces slowly. He finished the fight in two punches. One was a chopping left that knocked the instructor's guard down. The other was a right that landed on Parker's jaw like an axe on tough wood. Jim winced involuntarily at the sound of it. He knew that Hank, when he hit as hard as he could, was actually dangerous.

For Parker, the world exploded. His arms dropped as if all the tendons had been cut. His mouth flew open and his eyes rolled back. Then he shuddered in every fiber as if he were having a spasm, and began to topple forward.

Unnoticed on the outer edge, Crawford's head and shoulders loomed above the crowd. He had watched the whole fight intently, but Hank's knock-out punch seemed to take him by surprise. For a moment he looked discouraged and unhappy. Then his face brightened. For Parker did not fall. He was in a clinch with Hank and the two were wrestling each other around the ring.

"Good boy, Hank," murmured the Air Service Chief. "But it was awful close." Motioning to Stemple to follow him, he tramped back to the office. "Understand," he said, "as far as we're concerned, this scrap never happened."

Stemple met his look and nodded. "How you figure these things out is beyond me, though."

In these same moments, the fight was reaching its strange climax. Into that one shattering punch, Hank had put all his anger for two weeks of rough treatment, all his disgust at the way Parker had bullied Wimpy. But when it had landed, his rage was gone.

Just as in the plane when Wimpy couldn't jump, he had another instantaneous flash of understanding. He saw Lefty Parker not as the man who had sneered at him for two weeks but as the first smoke-jumper in history to walk the aerial road to a fire. He saw Lefty Parker as the instructor who, whatever his methods, had taught them all the tricks of the smokejumper's risky trade. He saw Lefty Parker as a fighter who could take punishment as well as dish it out. If there had been a single yellow fiber in Parker he would have found some way to call off the battle before now. Hank saw, finally, that if the fight ended with the instructor's being knocked out by a green recruit, Parker's career was done. He'd be jeered out of Air Service.

Lefty's nervous system was momentarily paralyzed, and he hung in Hank's arms completely helpless. But by wrestling him around, Hank made it look as if they were fighting in a clinch.

"Finish it, blast you," gasped Parker in his ear.

"Play up, work those hands," Hank retorted. "You'll be all right in a second."

A superb body in perfect condition reacted. The glassy look went out of Parker's eyes, life came back into his muscles. He was dizzy and weak, but he could stand when Hank pushed away from him saying, "How about calling it a round? I'm all in."

No one realized as they walked side by side out of the arena and sat down under a tree that Hank was practically carrying the instructor. The crowd disintegrated, now that the excitement was over. And not for weeks would the arguments end as to whether or not Hank could have stood up to Parker another round. A few rebels who advanced the notion that Hank was knocking Parker's block off were quickly laughed to silence. That was just plain idiotic.

"Kind of stepped out of my class, didn't I?" said Parker. He spoke laboriously, as if his tongue were swollen.

"Don't feel too bad about it," grunted Jim Dade. "You only tackled the intercollegiate heavyweight co-champion. Champion if he hadn't let a Navy man go just like he did you."

"Why?" asked Parker simply. "I had it coming. Why didn't you finish?"

"Oh, I don't know," replied Hank uneasily. "I got mad on account of you beating up poor old Wimpy. Then I just punched it out of my system, I guess." This was as close as Hank could come to explaining an act of pure generosity.

"Well, thanks anyway for not making a patsy out of me in front of the whole school." said Parker.

"But it's going to be a rough old road if I have to fight you every time I try to get rid of Wimpy. D'you guys still think he's a smokejumper?"

Like a thunderstorm, the fight had cleared the air. Hank could see now, for instance, that Parker's methods might be heavy-handed but they weren't all wrong. However much you sympathized with him and liked him, a man who refused his first jump and fainted on his second try was no parachutist.

Parker continued, "Tell you what I'll do. If you'll quit egging Wimpy on, I'll figure out a way to keep him in the outfit. He's a worker and he's good with his hands. They'll snap at him in the parachute loft as a rigger. And that's no second-rate job either. When I step out of a plane, I like to feel sure my canopy's going to open."

"Oh, that's swell," said Hank. "That clears up everything."

✤ NINE ✤

IT WAS amazing, the change that came over Parker's class after Wimpy left. He had been more of a drag on the others than they realized, and a constant irritation like a nail in a boot sole or a poorly balanced pack. His empty bed in the bunk house would have mocked them but for one thing. Wimpy was better off, too.

With a tact no one suspected, Parker had arranged it so that Stemple and Hank took Wimpy to apply for a job as parachute rigger. According to Hank, who could mimic people to the life when he chose, the scene had gone like this:

The parachute loft foreman, a crusty little old gnome, said incredulously, "You actually *want* to be a rigger, young feller?"

"Yes, sir," replied Wimpy, with his anxious grin.

Said the foreman, "It's a cruel hard life. You spend hours packing these chutes so neat an' pretty for them hoodlums to tear up an' drag through the mud in five minutes. Think you kin stand the monotony an' the injustice of it, young feller?"

"I think so."

"I do too," said the foreman in an entirely different tone. "Spotted you the day you toured the loft and you all tried your hands at folding a parachute. Any bonehead kin jump out of an airyplane but it takes a feller with sense t' pack a chute. Yours would have opened."

Always outstanding in spite of its handicaps, Lefty Parker's class fairly burned up the second half of smokejumper school. They still worked out on the jump tower and the let-down apparatus and the obstacle course. But the emphasis was on other things now, with just enough physical conditioning to keep them honed to razor edge sharpness.

They began to realize a fact that had been dinned into their ears from the first day: that in the end a parachutist is only a smokechaser with wings. But the array of skills an aerial smokechaser had to possess was astounding. Besides knowing all the standard methods of firefighting, he had to be able to splint an arm or apply a tourniquet or treat for shock. He had to be able to read a map as an ordinary person reads a book, to be as direction-wise as a homing pigeon—using a compass instead of his instinct. He had to be a radio technician, telephone repairman, tool sharpener, mechanic and weather observer all rolled into one. It was not enough to walk the aerial road to a smoke, find the fire after he was on the ground and put it out. The firefighter then had to sit down and write a report on exactly how he did it.

As second-year men who had been through all this before, Hank and Jim were somewhat disdainful at first until they discovered how much a man could forget in a winter. Then it was like old times to wrangle over the Fire Control Handbook, those hundred information-crammed pages better known as the "Smokechaser's Bible."

Outwardly things went on much as they had before. Parker still drove the class like a mule skinner with a balky team. But his tongue had lost its sting. The pupils understood now what the instructor was trying to do: cram the last possible bit of training into them before the hour when they stopped practicing and began playing for keeps.

After his most violent explosions, however, the victim was apt to return a too meek "Yes, teacher," and a grin.

And Parker was apt to grin back. After their second practice jump, he almost broke down and praised them to their faces.

The second jump was a descent into the forest with full firefighting equipment, and an artificial smoke as their objective. Parker started them off by planting the fire packs with uncanny accuracy in a tiny clearing that looked no larger than a handkerchief. When the plane made its second run over the target area and he led them out the door, they responded by following him so fast that six parachutes seemed to open at once.

Maneuvering like veterans, they all landed in the clearing so near each other that their canopies made a single pattern on the ground like a snowdrift. They had their tools unpacked and a fire line built around their "fire" before most of the instructors finished dragging their men out of the treetops and the creeks.

"That's smokejumping," said Parker as they lugged their equipment to the trucks waiting nearby. "Whether it's two at a time or a plane load. I don't go for this stringing men out all over a township and taking a day to round them up. Get down, get on the fire, get home. That's how to make smokejumping pay."

It was good reasoning, but Hank and Jim did not suspect that in eight words, Parker had foretold the greatest adventure of their lives.

That evening as they lazed on their bunks the recruits learned how soon the instructor's words would take on full meaning and this exciting game they were playing turn into grim reality.

Unnoticed by the others, in their usual quiet way, the twins were packing up. "Guess we won't be here for the graduation hop," said Rod.

"Huh? What?" came the startled response.

"Telegram from our boss," explained the other twin. "Fire season's early down there. We're pulling out tonight. Sure would like to see that graduation, though."

"Why? What's special about it?"

"Hadn't you heard? Some big wheels from Washington are coming to see it. Crawford's going to pull his mass jump for them. The latest thing in Air Service, a full hundred-man crew, complete down to the cook's flunky. Never even tried before. Well, make it pretty for us."

It seemed almost too casual, just to shake hands and say good-by after all they'd been through together. To Hank, at least, the moment offered a glimpse of the inner working of the Forest Service, a legion so big and so well organized that it could reach out two thousand miles for a pair of smoke-jumpers.

"You know," he said to Jim after the twins had gone, "I wonder why they're putting on such a big show. Must be some reason for it."

"Ah, you and your imagination," scoffed Jim. "They're just trying to sell somebody some proposition or other. Aren't they always? Your old man is probably one of the big wheels."

"Oh I know that," answered Hank. "He wrote me he'd be here. But it doesn't add up. They don't have to sell him on the Forest Service. You know as well as I do they're sticking their necks out to pull something brand-new in front of the brass. Suppose we foul it up? I smell trouble."

"You'll smell knuckles if you don't shut up and go to sleep," growled Jim.

✤ T E N ✤

∞∞∞∞∞∞∞∞∞∞∞∞∞∞∞∞∞∞∞∞∞∞

WHERE timbered hillsides loom above a certain valley in Montana there is a marvelous natural phenomenon. It is an almost perfect amphitheater, ringed on three sides by low ridges, its open end facing the valley. The floor of the amphitheater is a level meadow of grass, bright against the somber green of the forest of fir and spruce and pine. In rising tiers behind it tower the snow-capped battlements of the main range of the Rockies.

You would think Nature knew that one day men would need such a place at the edge of the wilderness and built it with one titanic scoop of her hand. It is a perfect flying field, protected on three sides from the violent mountain winds, and open on the fourth for the landing and take-off of airships.

Tourists whizzing along the transcontinental highway are often startled to hear a plane roar overhead, seemingly right out of the mountainside. Few of them notice the sign marking the entrance to the amphitheater. In modest green and white it reads: "SMOKEJUMPER BASE AIRFIELD, U. S. FOREST SERVICE." Few of them would know what a smokejumper is, anyway.

But on this June morning, quite a number of people had found the road to the hidden flying field. They stood in a close group. Some carried press cameras, others had wads of yellow copy paper sticking out of their pockets. It was obvious that most were spectators. At the moment their attention was focussed on a man in a Forest Service uniform.

Very tall, his face tempered by mountain wind and sun to the color of saddle leather, Air Service Chief Crawford was answering questions that beat on him excitedly from all sides.

"What you are about to see," he was explaining, "is forest fire-control history. For several years we have been using parachute firefighters in small numbers, two, three or four at the most, on small fires. That was during the test years of aerial fire control, and their success has been spectacular. The smoke-jumpers will go on stamping out the fires while they're small. But now, with greater responsibilities and more men, the Air Service is taking the next step, mass attack on large fires. The——"

"Let me ask a question, Mr.—er—Crawford," interrupted a voice. It had the sonorous roll of a practiced orator and issued from a pompous-looking man on the inner edge of the circle. Even into those few words he managed to put a feeling of antagonism. "Is the Forest Service actually considering using these—er—smokejumpers on a large scale and in place of established firefighting methods?"

"Yes, Senator Donahue," replied Crawford. "As of today, the smokejumper unit takes over complete fire responsibility for a million-and-a-half acres of the most inaccessible wilderness on this continent. Within that area lie the headwaters of a dozen rivers; billions of board feet of timber; thousands of acres of grazing land; hundreds of miles of trout streams and lakes; game animals and birds past counting. A couple of hundred young fellows with parachutes are going to take over from the much larger ground-based organization we have had there."

"Isn't the training and equipment of these—er—smokejumpers a highly expensive proposition?" With his actor's voice, Senator Donahue could put a whole paragraph of disdain into a single "er."

"That's a matter of comparison, isn't it?" a third voice put in.

Gratefully Crawford faced the new speaker, a trim, alert man with hair and eyes almost exactly the same shade of steel gray. "That's correct, Senator Winton," said the forester. "Individually each smokejumper costs us plenty. But his effective range is two hundred miles and up, against a maximum of twenty for the firefighter traveling overland."

"Well, maybe so," grumbled Donahue. "I'm prepared to reserve judgment until I can get an opinion from my son, an experienced airman. Unfortunately he cannot join me until later in the summer. To me, frankly, this business looks impractical. Grandstand stuff. And you can quote me on that." The last remark was tossed in the direction of the reporters.

There was an uncomfortable pause. Crawford's face showed no change of expression, but his tan had become two shades darker.

"Tell us about today's program," prompted Senator Winton just as the silence became unbearable.

Crawford replied in a strained voice, "As a test of training and organization, we plan to deliver onto this field, completely equipped, the first air-borne hundred-man firefighting crew in history. The smokejumper school's graduating class and instructors will put on the demonstration. When . . . ."

Crawford broke off, sensing some happening that had caught the attention of his audience. A glance over his shoulder told him what it was.

The empty meadow behind him had come to life. From every quarter, in groups of five and ten, men were filing toward the waiting planes—the smokejumpers. They looked like nothing earthly. Each wore a jump suit of heavy canvas, leather and steel reinforced to protect him from the shock of landing in anything from the top of a hundred-foot tree to a heap of boulders. Uuder the bulky parachute packs on chest and shoulders, the jump harness made a crisscross pattern. Their belts were hung with a variety of odd tools, and their pockets bulged with them.

There was no military precision to the advance of the smokejumpers, though they looked like soldiers from some strange planet. They strolled casually along, each squad to itself, with plenty of joking and horseplay. Yet, like a part of their equipment, they wore an air of self-reliance and purpose that was almost frightening. And they came by it honestly, as any man could attest who had ever seen a smokejumper bail out over the wildest, roughest country in North America.

"Pretty fair-looking outfit of men, wouldn't you say?" remarked Crawford in a conversational tone.

Most of the smokejumpers appeared to be eighteen or nineteen, except for some of the squad leaders and instructors. *They* might be old men of twenty-five. In a team passing near the group of spectators, Hank Winton towered over his fellows. Jim Dade was beside him, moving at his boxer's sliding gait and swinging his long arms.

A glance of recognition passed between Hank and his father, but no other sign. Jim, who was a party to the secret, didn't appear to look that way at all. But he caught the expression of consternation on Senator Winton's face before it was masked. He was about to question Hank about it when he decided it was none of his business. Instead he asked, "Who's the old goat next to your dad—the one got up like a comic cartoon of a politician?"

Hank peered and then began to chuckle. "The person you refer to as an old goat," he replied, "is none other than the Honorable Terence Aloysius Donahue, Senator of the United States."

"No fooling?" Jim stared frankly at the man standing beside the slender figure of Hank's father. Senator Donahue was portly, with a very red face and very white hair. As Jim had noticed, he was dressed in the cartoonist's uniform for a politician: striped gray trousers, flowing cutaway coat, black string tie and wide-brimmed hat.

"Does he have to dude up like that? Never saw your father in any such rig."

"That'd be the day," laughed Hank. "I guess in Donahue's state they go in for it."

For a few paces they trudged along in silence. "I tell you what," said Hank suddenly. "There's so much brass around, we ought to give them their money's worth."

Jim glanced at his companion suspiciously. A college term as Hank's roommate and almost as a member of the Winton family had made him wary. Hank's sense of humor was apt to run to violence. Jim questioned him with his eyes.

"If the jump pattern worked out, we could land sort of close to them. Get 'em to run a little, maybe," explained Hank.

"Your dad wouldn't." Any further reply Jim might have made was drowned by the angry bellow of many airplane motors warming up. Once inside their ship there was no further chance to talk. The cabin was crammed to the roof with men and equipment. Already most of the other smokejumpers had put on their steel-latticed helmets. Jim, with his own poised, gave Hank a long, slow look and shook his head.

At this instant the plane lurched forward and began to sway as it ran across the meadow. In silence, looking now completely like creatures from a different planet, the smokejumpers took to the air.

✸ ELEVEN ✸

THE SMOKEJUMPER planes had circled far out over the valley, almost out of sight. Now, flying straight and true for the amphitheater, they were coming back in a long, widely spaced column.

Air Service Chief Crawford had moved the audience back to the edge of the trees. Now he spoke again: "Under actual conditions a crew coming in to tackle a big fire would be scattered, a squad here and a squad there, along the perimeter. For demonstration purposes we're going to land the entire outfit on this field, organize and set up a fire camp for your inspection.

"The equipment comes down first, marked by colored streamers. Each squad uses its equipment as a jump target. First man out, incidentally, will be John Stemple, the fire boss."

"That's something new," remarked one of the reporters. "The general lands ahead of his army."

A ripple of comment ran through the group, but no man lowered his eyes. The lead plane was coming in now, drilling a straight line a thousand feet above the field. All could see the black opening in its side. They heard the steady drone of its engines die away momentarily and at that instant three bundles shot out from the doorway. Supported on small cargo chutes, trailing long, gaudy streamers, they rapidly fell straight down. With a triple thud they landed near the closed end of the amphitheater, a hundred yards from the spectators.

Already the plane was banking. As it came overhead on its second pass, every man on the ground involuntarily held his breath. Each one could see the doll-sized human figure poised in the black doorway. Each one was imagining himself up there with the wind wrenching at his body, with nothing between him and a thousand feet of emptiness but a thin canopy of nylon.

The engine noise faded. Then, as rapidly as a man could count, ten smokejumpers tumbled out of the plane. Their opening parachutes were ten evenly spaced explosions of white against the sky. In the quiet air the reports were sharp as rifle fire.

Unseen by the rest of the audience, a message in the lift of an eyebrow and the faint nod of a head passed between Air Service Chief Crawford and Senator Winton. Very few people, certainly not Donahue, knew that a senator's son dangled beneath one of those white canopies. Crawford's nod had told the father that his son was safe. The senator's tightly clenched hands slowly relaxed in his pockets.

For a few moments the smokejumpers appeared to be suspended in mid air. Then the onlookers realized that their tiny figures were growing larger by the second and that they were drifting farther apart.

"You'll see real parachute work now," remarked Crawford. "They're going to land as close to the equipment as they can without getting in each other's way. With our Forest Service maneuverable parachute, in still air like this a good jumper can just about sit down on his own sleeping bag."

Even while he was speaking, the watchers could note one jumper who had drifted some distance from his mates. He was close enough now so that they could see him manipulate the guide lines running down from the steering slots in his canopy. They could even see the slots open. Then the jumper made an almost level dart across the sky to rejoin his group.

The spectators began to break away from the group and move forward to see better. The smoke-jumpers were very close now. They looked enormous, and their faceless heads were all bent toward the earth. Seen at close range, their descent was very swift, almost like falling. Most of the watchers halted, and some began to retreat. Only Senator Donahue continued his advance.

"Better hold it," called Crawford. "Those boys come in pretty fast!"

Donahue paid no attention. No smokejumper, the set of his jaw seemed to say, had better land on him.

It was at this moment that a stray puff of wind meandering over the field seized one canopy and tugged it playfully aside. For a moment the chutist streamed out behind it, directly over the audience. Instantly he righted himself and with a jerk on his guide lines began to swing toward open ground again.

Senator Donahue's first warning was the whine of

air in the steering slots. He looked up to see an armored monster plunging at him with terrifying speed. With a bellow of fear and all his pomposity deflated, he began to run.

"Stand still," called Crawford. "Give him a chance."

Donahue paid no attention to this advice, either. He ran as a fat man runs, body leaning back, arms pumping, knees high, feet pawing at the earth. Like bombs, smokejumpers began to land on all sides of him. Desperately the Senator zigzagged, for one monster, more gigantic than the rest, still pursued him.

Hank Winton, for it was Hank, watched the fleeing man narrowly. He had regained control of his chute and thought that if that idiot on the ground stood still or even ran in a straight line, it would be a cinch to miss him.

There were split seconds to go now. In the very last, Hank calmly invited a broken leg by cracking open his steering slots. The chute jerked him violently to one side, and he hit the ground two yards from Donahue.

It was a hard landing, awkward and off balance.

At the moment of contact, Hank was actually traveling backward. A thick-set jumper, who had already landed and opened the quick-release buckle on his harness, ran frantically toward Hank, trying to throw himself onto the shroud lines of Hank's parachute and keep him from being dragged. But trained reflexes and an iron-hard body met the shock and converted it into a roll.

Hank turned two complete backward somersaults and ended standing up.

The senator still ran, unconscious that the danger was over. In grotesque slow motion he and the collapsing parachute came together. The gleaming, supple folds descended upon him and muffled his last wild cry. Then the white mound began to twist and leap and squirm as if it had a life of its own.

The silence lasted only a moment. Then someone chuckled. Somebody else laughed out loud. A choking voice cried, "Just like a trout. I can't stand it." Senator Winton managed to look amused and worried both at the same time. Crawford strode forward, his face a mask though the muscles in his flat cheeks were twitching.

Hank and Jim were ahead of everyone else. They

seized one edge of the parachute and rolled it back until the trapped senator was uncovered. The first part of him to appear was his face, now the color of a ripe tomato.

"I'm terribly sorry, sir," said Hank in a voice muffled by his helmet. "If only you hadn't run."

"You insolent young fool," roared Senator Donahue, "you did this on purpose! You might have crippled me."

Jim tore off his helmet to reveal a face almost as red as the senator's. "You mean he nearly crippled himself saving you, you——"

"Jim."

There was probably only one voice in the world that could halt hot-tempered Jim Dade. That voice spoke now, quietly but sharp as the crack of a whip. "Too bad this happened," Crawford continued. "But there's no harm done."

"Now Donahue, remember your blood pressure," admonished Hank's father, seeing the senator's mouth open for another roar. "You look just like a Roman emperor in that toga effect." And then in a lower voice, "Get hold of yourself. The press is watching, maybe taking pictures."

"Deliberate attempt to humiliate me," jabbered Donahue. "No more than I expected——" his voice became anguished. "What? Photographs? Oh, no." Dragging Senator Winton after him, he hurried away. His orator's voice could be heard booming, "No photographs of this unfortunate accident. Please, gentlemen of the press. It would spoil this fine demonstration."

"The show goes on," said Crawford.

And so it did. Another set of orange cargo streamers already lay on the ground. The second plane was disappearing over the nearest ridge, leaving behind its daisy chain of parachutes. Out above the valley, the third was leveling off for its run. Behind it, circling watchfully, were a fourth and a fifth.

With a significant glance at Hank's father, Crawford said to the smokejumpers, "You two have a dinner date in town. I guess we can get through the inspection of the fire camp and equipment without you. Now hightail it out of here."

Gratefully, Hank and Jim hightailed it.

✤ TWELVE ✤

〰〰〰〰〰〰〰〰〰〰〰〰〰〰〰〰

"IF YOU ever do a thing like that again, I'll beat your brains out with your own jump belt," Jim warned in his abrupt way.

"Huh?" said Hank Winton blankly.

"What do you mean, Jim?" added Senator Winton.

"Why sir, dynamiting his chute that way just before a landing, he should have broken both legs, or cracked his skull." Jim paused for a moment, his dark, almost sullen face tense with concentration. When he went on it was obviously a heroic effort, as if something long unsaid were forcing its way out of him. "I'll lose my mind worrying over the big lug. He's always stepping into punches aimed at somebody else, like he did with Parker. Like today.

Like with me—after the hard time I gave him last year. I don't understand such people."

This was probably the closest touchy, independent Jim Dade would ever come to speaking of the previous summer. Jim, an orphan who had fought his way up literally with his fists, and Hank, the offspring of wealth and power, had waged a season-long feud that nearly cost both of them their careers as foresters. It had taken encirclement in a great forest fire to make them friends.

Their shared experience had changed both of them. Some of Jim's fierce ambition had entered easygoing Hank. And some of Hank's good nature had softened Jim's bellicose attitude toward the world.

The senator groped for something to say or do to ease the tension. Things were getting uncomfortably close to sentiment. But it was Hank who saved the moment.

He raised a forkful of apple pie and ice cream to his lips and then lowered it again. "I can't swallow it," he said in tones of pain and astonishment.

"A pitiful thing," replied his father solemnly. "And only your third helping." Then he and Jim burst into laughter that rang all through the huge hotel dining room. More than one person looked their way, envying people who could laugh like that.

"Speaking of aviation," said Hank's father presently, "I'd appreciate a summary of what goes on here. When you two left last month, you expected to go back to Three Rivers District and spend another summer on lookout towers, combing lightning bolts out of your whiskers. That was the routine for a couple of second-year men, as I got it. Now I find you jumping out of airplanes, waving nylon bedspreads. In short, what cooks, fellers?"

Hank replied, "That's out of date, Pop. Things don't cook any more. They clobber. You see, Crawford was leaving Three Rivers for Air Service and taking Stemple with him. And you know Jim and I made that emergency jump last year over on the Sacajawea Forest. So we just naturally wound up in smokejumper school."

Senator Winton looked at Jim Dade pleadingly. "That's probably the briefest summary on record. Suppose you tell it, Jim, with more detail and if possible, coherently."

Jim took up the story: "When we reported in at

headquarters, they sent us down to Crawford's office. We figured, of course, he'd be on the district that late in spring. At first we couldn't make out what was going on. The boss told us that the Forest Service is big and complicated, and that anyone intending to work his way up has to have a specialty along with all-around experience. He said we should start preparing right now, even though we've got years of regular field work ahead. I forget all the things he mentioned: Timber Management, Grazing Management, Research, Engineering, Recreation, Wildlife. When he got to Forest Fire Control, we told him he could stop.

"So that's the way it happened. He told us Air Service has been so successful experimentally that they're going in for it on a big scale. The smoke-jumpers are taking over entirely on one big Primitive Area, a million and a half acres of the wildest country there is. Three Rivers, our old stamping ground, is right in the middle of it. The big shots wanted him to come in as Chief of Air Service and he told them he would if he could take along the men he wanted from the district. For example, John Stemple; Ben Gray, his dispatcher; and half a dozen of his smokechasers, including us.

"Well, that's it. If he wanted us, we sure didn't give him time to change his mind."

The senator nodded understanding. "I don't see how you could make a mistake by following Crawford. Now, a question on a slightly different topic. For my own information, was that performance out at the field this afternoon an accident or something you two devils cooked—I mean clobbered up?"

Hank squirmed under the penetrating eye of his father. "Cross my heart, it was an accident," he said. "Earlier I did have some idea of giving you a scare. But Jim wouldn't go for it. What happened was I caught a gust in my chute. I didn't even know who was under me until I was right on top of him. Anyway, the clown had no business running."

"Son," reproved the senator. "Besides, you're wrong. Whatever Donahue may be, it's not a clown. That comic supplement getup is camouflage. Actually there's no man in politics more dangerous or, figuratively, quicker on his feet. But he does have one special weakness."

"What's that?"

"No sense of humor. And that's what makes this

business serious. Deliberately or not, you've done the one thing to Donahue that he can never forgive. You've made him look foolish in public."

"Gosh," said Hank soberly. "You mean he might get us in bad with the Forest Service."

Senator Winton shook his head. "That's the least of it. Donahue is after bigger game. I hoped I wouldn't have to tell you this, but now you'll have to know. Senator Donahue and I are out here on a full-dress investigation of the Forest Service. Donahue's idea. I forced myself onto the committee in order to keep an eye on things."

"Investigation!" cried Hank and Jim together.

Hank's father chuckled. "Don't look so tragic, boys. It isn't the end of the world. Investigation is a necessary part of government, goes on all the time and does a lot of good. Any large organization needs to be prodded occasionally, even your Forest Service.

"A fair inquiry will do your outfit no harm. On the contrary, it will end by silencing some of its enemies. Of which the Forest Service has plenty."

Senator Winton had the rapt attention of his audience. In his sharp, precise way he was giving the two young foresters a glimpse of the forces that moved behind the scenes.

"Enemies," snorted Jim belligerently. "I know what kind."

"Yes," nodded the senator. "The envious, the selfish and the ignorant, mostly. People who resent being told, 'Thou shalt not burn, waste and destroy.' Also some like Donahue, professional troublemakers.

"Now understand me. Donahue is an able man. He's had twenty years in public life based on his investigations. He's uncovered some situations that needed to be uncovered. The only really objectionable thing about him is his motive. What he does is not for the good of the country, but for the glory of Donahue."

"I still don't see why he has to pick on the Forest Service," argued Hank.

"Because it's big and powerful. Because it has enemies. Because right now it's engaged in something new and radical," retorted the Senator. "To you, smokejumping is just a practical and advanced way of getting a job done. Most people don't see beyond the spectacular part of it. All of which boils down to a formula a professional faultfinder can smell in Washington, D. C."

"Well then, you run Donahue off," suggested Hank confidently. "You pack plenty of voltage yourself, Pop."

The Senator shook his head regretfully. "Not that much, I'm afraid. This affair started out as routine. Donahue had no peeve against the Forest Service. He'd have made a fuss over some unimportant things—there's always a little dead wood in a big tree—got himself into the headlines, and that would have been the end of it. Standard technique in an election year.

"But now he's angry. And when he's angry, Donahue loses all sense of proportion."

"You mean he'd do something against the whole Forest Service just because a couple of two-bit smokejumpers bothered him?" asked Hank incredulously.

"Exactly. That's the trouble with a man with no sense of humor. In his present mood, Donahue is capable of wrecking the Forest Service. He's got me to deal with first, of course. But I want you two to stay out of his way. No matter what happens."

✣ THIRTEEN ✣

A PAIR of very subdued smokejumpers walked along the softly lighted streets of Midvale, Montana. They were faced with a problem new in their experience. The heart-stopping moment when a man plunges out of his plane and waits for his chute to open, the bitter struggle to tame a forest fire, the weary hike back to the base through a trackless wilderness—those were honest dangers. A man could face them squarely. But this underground maneuvering, there was no way to get your hands on it.

Said Hank gloomily, "I still can't believe Donahue would dry-gulch the whole Forest Service just because of something that happened by accident. Nobody in his right mind would carry a grudge that far."

"Read history," growled Jim. "It's full of characters that flipped their lids for no good reason and dragged everything down just to hear the thud."

"Maybe it would help if I went and apologized to him."

"Apologize? To a bird that's looking for trouble? All you can do is kick his teeth in—or keep out of his way like your dad told us. Let him handle Donahue. He can give that windbag the worst day he ever saw."

It was impossible for Hank Winton to remain gloomy very long. Jim's practical slant cheered him up at once. He said, "You're right. At least it won't be any trouble keeping out of Donahue's way. He won't be jumping on many fires. Well, let's drag the bodies up to the warehouse and find a couple of bye-bye sacks. Too late to catch a ride back to base now."

Midvale, Montana is a city girdled by mountains. The riches of those mountains built it. The caulked boots of the logger, the high heels of the cattleman, the hobnails of the miner all play their distinctive tunes on its sidewalks.

And Midvale is also a Forest Service town, headquarters of a region, a wilderness empire five hundred miles long and two hundred wide. Here are its offices, shops and warehouses, its remount depot, radio station, airfields and laboratories. Patiently Hank and Jim had explained this to Senator Winton when the latter offered to send them by taxi the twenty miles back to the smokejumper base. The idea horrified them. In a Forest Service town no forester needs to look far for lodging, meals and transportation.

"Let's stop in here a minute," said Jim all at once.

"Here?" Hank looked doubtful. Jim had turned toward a doorway over which a neon sign read "Jonesey's Place." It was a combined tavern, luncheonette and pool hall. "What would we want in there?"

"Want you to meet a friend of mine, the only real one I had for a long time."

As the two smokejumpers entered, a remarkable figure came to meet them. It was a Negro, black as charcoal, with a fuzz of white hair like a halo around his bald pate. He was built somewhat along Jim's lines, stocky but with even broader shoulders and longer arms. Plainly an old man, he still moved with catlike grace and power.

"Jim boy, good to see you," he cried in softest southern dialect.

"Good to see you, Jonesey," replied Jim. Playfully he aimed a punch at the old Negro's head. Involuntarily Hank flinched, for Jim's playful punches traveled at the speed of a thrown baseball.

What followed was almost incredible. The Negro picked the blow out of the air as a magician picks a coin, and converted it into a handshake.

"Haven't lost your timing, I see," laughed Jim. "Hank, I want you to meet Benjamin Franklin Jones, better known as the Black Leopard, the greatest middleweight of all time. He taught me all I know about boxing. Used to get me fights."

"You'd have been champeen, a few moh yeahs," replied the old fighter seriously. "Boy, you had it all. But no mind, the Foh-rest Service is a bettah thing . . . Pleased to meet you, Mistah Hank. You Foh-rest Service too?"

"He is," said Jim. "Think we could make a box fighter of him, Jonesey?"

Hank felt the diamond eyes of the Black Leopard burn into him like flames.

"Yeah man," stated the Negro. "But foh one thing. You's too good-natuhed, big fellah."

"Just right," crowed Jim. "Only the other day he was taking a guy apart who really had it coming, and then——"

All along Hank had been conscious of the hum of conversation in the crowded little tavern, the click of billiard balls and the clatter of glasses. And gradually rising above the general din, a voice that grew louder and louder. It was a bad-tempered Donahue sort of voice, but without that old pirate's elegance. Standing close to Jim, Hank felt him stiffen when that voice pronounced: "——Forest Service thinks it runs everything west of the Mississippi. Graze your cattle here, don't graze them there. Do this; don't do that. Everything goes by the book. It's time we took those brass monkeys and fed them their book of regulations a page at a time with their tin badges for a chaser."

A chorus of, "You bet; that's telling 'em; you said it," followed this outburst.

Jim spun round as if something had stung him, and a wave of red surged up his neck. He could be as impatient as anyone with red tape and brass— among other foresters. But no outsider had that privilege. Across six feet of smoky air, Jim faced the speaker. He was a beefy, sunburned individual, dressed in typical rancher style: high-heeled riding boots, frontier pants, Stetson hat. In his group he was apparently a leader by right of the loudest voice, if nothing else.

"Jim," whispered Hank urgently. "Let it go. Don't start anything here." He felt a little sick at his stomach. He had believed it when his father told him that the Forest Service had enemies. But this naked hostility made it real and personal. His impulse was to get away from there and let the thin, sharp odor of the wilderness cut the fumes out of his nostrils.

Jim apparently didn't hear him. He minced toward the rancher on the balls of his feet, like a cat on a wet floor, muttering, "I know that big baboon. Where was it?" Then he said aloud, "Something in particular you don't like about the Forest Service, or just everything in general?"

"And what would that be to you, bub?" retorted the rancher.

Around the two hostile voices, silence gathered. There were curious stares and a gradual movement inward.

"This punk bothering you, boss?" a lanky cow-puncher shouldered his way into the circle and looked contemptuously down at Jim.

Without turning his head, Jim snapped, "Hank, keep this cow nurse off my back while I take care of a little unfinished business. I remember now. Last summer you felt different about the Forest Service, when that trash fire you started got away and went into your grain. You bawled for the Forest Service then, like a calf. That's all you ever do, it looks like. Bawl."

The cattleman's face turned muddy with rage. "You're safe," he growled thickly, "talking from behind a badge."

Very deliberately Jim unpinned the tiny shield of the Forest Service and pretended to put it into his pocket. At that moment, when his hands were down, the rancher struck viciously, left and right.

His attack was suicidal. Without moving his feet, Jim rocked smoothly forward and inside the clumsy blows. With his left hand he pushed the towering rancher off balance while his right completed its trip to his pocket. Then he struck his counter-blow. The punch traveled about eight inches, so hard and fast that the rancher stiffened as if he had taken a bullet between the eyes. All his joints seemed to come apart as he fell.

Simultaneously, the cowpuncher launched a kick at Jim's back that would have crippled him if it had landed. Until then Hank had hoped that the quarrel might pass off with nothing more than loud words. As Jonesey had detected, he was too good-natured ever to make a natural fighter. But underneath that friendliness drowsed a temper, honestly inherited. Parker could have warned the cowboy not to set it off.

With that cowardly attack on his partner from behind, Hank simply exploded. The kick never reached its target. As Jonesey met Jim's punch, Hank caught it in mid flight. An upward heave of his shoulders converted the kick into a grotesque, sprawling high jump. And as the cowpuncher slowly spun in mid air, Hank's iron knuckles turned his face into a gory mask. He lay quietly where he fell, like a sack.

A mob is unpredictable in every reaction but one. It is always hungry for blood. This one was prejudiced besides. A voice yelled, "Take the Forest Service punks." Instantly Jim and Hank disappeared in a storm of flailing arms and fists.

But as mobs have never been able to understand, a couple of trained fighters, battling as a unit, are no easy prey. Deadly and silent as a pair of wolves surrounded by yapping dogs, Hank and Jim met the unorganized assault. They fought back to back, taking plenty of punishment but dealing out ten times as much.

When the riot squad came they were almost the only people in the tavern except Jonesey still on their feet. Throughout the fight the old champion had stood guard over his cash register apparently undisturbed by the odds against his young visitors.

"Big fellah," he said as a policeman led a battered Hank out the door, "I was wrong about you. All you needs is to git mad."

✢ FOURTEEN ✢

MISERABLY Hank and Jim faced Crawford across the desk in his tiny office. They were bruised, rumpled and grimy. A night in the Midvale city jail had taken all the gleam from their exploit so that even Jim had lost his normal air of independence. Too late they began to realize that they had involved the Forest Service in a public brawl, exactly what Hank's father had warned them not to do. A glance at the headlines of the newspaper spread on Crawford's desk was enough to tell them that. They had given Senator Donahue another opening for an attack on the Forest Service.

Hank felt as if the words were printed on his brain:

SMOKEJUMPERS WRECK LOCAL TAVERN

He looked hopefully at Stemple, who had brought them from the jail, but Stemple's gloomy face was averted. He looked at Crawford and could not read his expression.

The Air Service Chief said, "Well, you two young roosters seem to have made quite a showing. Suppose you tell me about it."

"I started the roughhouse. Just leave Hank out of it," blurted Jim.

"Nobody told me I had to stay there," retorted Hank instantly. "I was in it just as much as Jim."

"You look it," observed Crawford dryly. "And never mind trying to protect each other. Just tell me what happened."

So, as Jim maintained a sullen silence, Hank told the story of the fight. When he was finished, he realized that Crawford was silently laughing.

"Quite an affair," he commented. "Now, we're going up to the old man's office. For some reason unknown to me, the higherups are interested in your scuffle. When we get there, all I want to hear out of you is Yes or No, and not that unless you're spoken to."

They were going to be hauled up before the Regional Forester himself. Hank's knees quaked as he went out of the office. But Crawford was on their side. He knew that now, without being told it in so many words, and the knowledge gave him courage.

Neither Hank nor Jim heard Crawford's urgent aside to Stemple as he followed them: "Get this man Jones and keep him handy."

The two smokejumpers attempted a bold entrance into the Regional Forester's office. But their brave front faded when they discovered a whole room full of people waiting for them. In his first startled glance Hank identified Manley, the Regional Forester; Morrow, the Regional Fire Chief; and his father. A secretary was at one corner of Manley's desk busily taking notes, and off to one side was one of the reporters who had been at the airfield.

A blast of sound beat on the ears of the smokejumpers, the organ voice of Senator Donahue with all stops out. "—have been dubious about this parachute business from the start. That incident at the airfield yesterday was inexcusable. It shows what happens when tried-and-true methods of doing things, controlling forest fires, for instance, are scrapped for something new and spectacular. And now it appears that this wonderful crew of—er— smokejumpers, charged with the responsibility of protecting our priceless national resources, is no more than a gang of hoodlums."

While this tirade thundered on and on, Hank and Jim had a chance to get hold of themselves. Hank's knees wouldn't stop their faint trembling, but he lost his kicked-dog expression. Instead of looking sullen and bewildered, Jim began to look angry.

Hank caught his father's eye and was amazed to receive a long, slow wink. Immediately the senator looked up at the ceiling with an expression of unconcern. It was an old signal between the two. It meant that for good and important reasons, they must go on pretending to be strangers.

It never entered Hank's mind that his father would deny him because he had been in a mob fight and had spent a night in jail. Things weren't handled that way in the Winton family. Hank decided that his father must be planning a surprise for

Donahue. His mind raced. That red-cheeked orator who was now working himself up to the climax of his speech undoubtedly knew that Senator Winton had a son. But they had never met.

That must be the answer, Hank decided. His father was going to let Donahue go too far to back out and then mention in his quiet, deadly way that it was a fellow senator's son he was calling a hoodlum. Senator Winton was a master of the art of letting an adversary destroy himself.

Regional Forester Manley sat staring straight ahead, his face expressionless. Fire Chief Morrow, on the other hand, was making no attempt to hide his impatience. Air Service Chief Crawford, with his chair tilted back against the wall, looked bored and half asleep. To anyone who knew him, this meant that he was furious and about as bored as a hungry tiger. To everybody in the room except Donahue it was known that to attack one of Crawford's men was to attack Crawford, and that was no mean undertaking.

"And I say to you high officials of the Forest Service," cried Donahue in a voice quivering with emotion, "as I shall have to say to my colleagues in the Senate, that no federal organization, no matter how great and powerful, will be permitted to do business in such a slipshod manner or keep such undesirable characters in its employ."

He had run down at last. Fire Chief Morrow's lips soundlessly formed the words: "And you can quote me on that." Crawford's eyes flew open. Now it's coming, thought Hank, watching his father.

But it was actually the Regional Forester who said mildly into the vast silence, "I think we should find out now what happened last night—before we pass judgment."

"You mean listen to a well-rehearsed alibi," sneered Donahue.

The legs of Crawford's chair hit the floor with a thump. Ignoring the pleading eye and hand signals of Manley, he rasped, "Just to keep the record straight, these two hoodlums were something else beginning with 'h' last year. This same newspaper called them heroes. Remember? They jumped on a fire—in the middle of the night—without previous parachute training. They saved approximately one hundred thousand acres of the finest timber in the northwest and nearly lost their lives in the process. Maybe we'd better start rehearsing our alibis."

"We'll need to question only one witness," said the Regional Forester hastily. He looked questioningly at Crawford, got a nod in answer, and turned to his secretary, saying, "Will you ask Mr. Jones to come in?"

From a connecting office, Benjamin Franklin Jones appeared with his huge grin and his catlike way of moving. He did not appear to be awed by the company. After all, the Black Leopard had fought before kings and princes and had shaken the hand of a president of the United States.

"Mistah Manley, suh," he said in his soft drawl, "Mistah Crawford and gennelmen. These heah boys was in mah place mindin' theah own business talkin' old times with me. Some loud-mouth begins abusin' theah outfit. Jim reminds him how one day the Foh-rest Service done him a good tuhn. Then Mistah Loud-mouth swang on Jim an' his buddy try to kick Jim in th' kidneys.

"That's how she staht, gennelmen. These boys didn' strike the first blow—but they suah struck the last. An' they got mah permission to clean that kinda riffraff outa mah place any time."

Gravely, Jonesey sat down. For several moments, no one said anything at all. Crawford tilted his chair back against the wall and closed his eyes again. But his lips were stretched in a wolfish grin. Fire Chief Morrow hid his face behind hands propped on his knees, but he could not hide the rocking of his shoulders. Senator Donahue had the shocked expression of a man who has swallowed a red-hot pepper by mistake.

The reporter, who had been scribbling furiously since the moment Crawford mentioned the night fire jump of the previous year, suddenly got to his feet. "Excuse me," he said hurriedly. "Got a dead-line to make. They'll have to rewrite the first page."

Donahue mumbled something of which the only audible word was "hasty."

Senator Winton broke in smoothly, "I'll recom-mend now what I suggested in the first place, when you invited us to take part in this inquiry. I still think it's the family business of the Forest Service, and no concern of ours. We'll just run along and let the Forest Service settle——"

The telephone on Manley's desk interrupted with its urgent clang. His secretary picked up the handset, listened a moment and then held it out to Crawford. "Air Service radio calling," she said.

The Air Service Chief was across the room in two long strides. "Crawford," he said into the mouthpiece. "Go ahead."

In the hush, the metallic voice of the telephone was audible throughout the room. Hank and Jim instantly recognized their old friend Ben Gray, Crawford's dispatcher.

"Report from the patrol plane, boss," said Ben. "He's trailing a lightning storm up Wolf River. All his jumpers are down and he's got eight more smokes spotted. I'm loading two squads now. Take-off in three minutes."

Crawford let the receiver drop onto its stand. "Come on, smokejumpers," he barked. "Time we got back on the job."

FIFTEEN

SIX WEEKS passed. Like signposts along a highway, newspaper headlines told their story:

SENATORIAL PROBE
Reveals Forest Service Inefficient

SMOKEJUMPERS QUELL FIRES

STOCKMEN FETE SENATE INVESTIGATORS
Forest Service Dictatorial Asserts Senator Donahue

LIGHTNING FIRES INCREASE
Smokejumpers Handle Record Number

PARACHUTE CHIEF GRILLED
Senator's Airman Son To Probe
Smokejumper Value

CANADA FIRE RAGES
U. S. Parachutists Scout Conflagration

In the middle of fire season, however, smoke-jumpers have little interest in headlines. They live in a world of their own, alternating between frantic activity and brief periods of waiting.

At the smokejumper base, two Air Service squad leaders whiled away such a period of inaction with idle conversation. Through an open door they could see into the bunk room where their men read or wrote letters, repaired equipment or catnapped. These were the normal activities of a smokejumper crew on call.

On the other side of the office was the communications center. Here radios gabbled and telephones rang incessantly, twenty-four hours a day, bringing reports from the vast wilderness lying invisible behind the summer haze. One hint of danger would transform the drowsy men in a matter of seconds into an expert fighting force moving to battle at two hundred miles an hour.

A squad leader of smokejumpers wears no distinctive badge or uniform. He looks, in fact, like any other smokejumper. But during the hours when his squad is on duty he has the privilege of having an office. He can stalk at any time into the communications room to riffle the file of reports at the dispatcher's elbow or study the fire-danger charts or the maps plastered on every wall.

He may be a little finer drawn than his men, a little thinner. When his plane levels off over a pillar of smoke in some trackless corner of the wilderness, he checks the static cord as each jumper poises himself in the open, windy door. He taps each jumper to start him on the long plunge to earth, grows a little older during each breathless wait while the jumper is in free fall. He breathes again when the huge white flower explodes from the parachute pack. There is no one to check *his* static cord, that strip of webbing that automatically opens a parachute, or tap *his* shoulder. The squad leader is the last man out, reserving for himself the toughest jumps and the hottest fires.

In two months of the aerial firefighter's strange life, Hank Winton and Jim Dade had won the privileges and the extra burdens of leadership. They had changed a little. Even when a boy is nineteen, responsibility can put a certain watchful look into his eyes, a certain air of maturity into every word and action.

The ranks of the smokejumpers had thinned a little since graduation day. Some couldn't stand the pace: bored with inaction one minute, driven to the limit of endurance the next. Some had been shipped to other regions, planes, parachutes and all, in response to pleas for help. A few were always laid up with the smokejumper's occupational disease, sprained ankles.

Those that were left had been tempered by many a rough landing. Their reinforced boots had touched on grassy meadows, on boulder-strewn hillsides and on mountain swamps. They had draped parachutes over alpine flower beds, brush jungles and the tops of towering trees from Canada to the desert. They were a tough outfit and proud of it.

"How d'you suppose old Senator Donahooey's getting along with his investigation?" asked Hank lazily.

Their skirmishes with that red-faced politician seemed faraway and unimportant now.

Jim, thumbing through a badly scribbled notebook, replied with a snort, "As long as he doesn't come sniffing around here, who cares?"

"I know, but it kind of irritates you to think of

him prying everywhere. It's like my dad said, you can always find some little thing to beef about."

"Feed him this for beef then," said Jim. "Do you realize that we've handled two hundred and thirty-eight fires, over half of them in that big flare-up the last of July? And not one of them ever got beyond Class B. In case you didn't know it, this is the worst year since 1910 for number of fires started and the best in history for number of fires held to less than one acre."

"Well, what did you expect?" demanded Hank. "Crawford and Stemple have this thing humming like a new airplane design . . . You know, it's funny how things turn out. Take old Donahue. He has a son who's a real guy, an army test pilot."

"You can have Donahue," sniffed Jim. "And his son, too. The son must take after his mother."

Hank doubled up with laughter. Incapable himself of holding a grudge for more than five minutes, Jim's reactions always amused him. When a person was in wrong with Jim, he was in wrong all over.

"Grin, you big ape," grumbled Jim. "I'm just glad your old man is trailing that Senate buddy of his around. With him on the lookout, Donahooey won't get away with a thing . . . Well, we're off in two hours. Let's go fishing."

Neither of the smokejumpers had noticed the arrival of two men in the communications center. With low-voiced comment, Crawford and Stemple were looking over the reports for the past twenty-four hours.

Ben Gray, the dispatcher whom Crawford had brought along from Three Rivers, looked up from the gleaming radio panels. Casually he said, "Got something here that might interest you, boss. Tuned in on a fire down in Idaho for a while this morning. They seem to be having quite a time."

"I know," replied Crawford without interest. "There's a good one going out on the coast too. John, aren't Bailey and Chadwick overdue?"

Stemple grinned. He firmly believed that if every smokejumper in the Air Service were out on a fire at one time, Crawford would know the location of each man to the quarter section and remember how long he had been gone to the hour.

"They reported at two this morning," he explained. "Telephone at their first check station was dead."

"I took the data on this Idaho deal," continued Gray imperturbably. "It's over there on the plotting table."

Crawford and Stemple looked at each other and then at the dispatcher. No one had ever seen Ben Gray excited or heard him raise his voice no matter what insanity beat at him by radio and telephone. But these three men had worked so long together under pressure that they could almost read each other's minds. Without being told, Gray and Stemple knew that more than anything else Crawford longed to put the outfit he had trained to the final test, a mass jump on a big fire.

Crawford dropped the report file. John followed him to a table where a brilliant light beat upon the intricate markings of a large map. Their eyes instantly focussed on a part of it where red dots made a pockmarked design.

To the mountain-wise observer, the coloring and markings described a wilderness of dense forest, towering peaks and deep canyons. "No roads, mighty few trails and plenty rough," interpreted Gray out loud.

The Air Service Chief said, "Well, they're doing

a messy job of control. With twenty or thirty fires inside a two-mile circle, will you please tell me why they're trying to fight each one individually? They'll end up by losing the whole business." His voice rose. "Ben, I could cut your heart out for this, letting me waste fifteen minutes on routine stuff while all the time you had this up your sleeve!"

His angry shout brought two inquisitive heads into the doorway. Hank and Jim listened, ready to duck in a moment if Crawford should turn their way.

"They hadn't lost the fire then," replied Gray calmly. "They have now, though."

Stemple looked inquiringly at the Air Service Chief, and his eyes were sparkling. "Us?" he said. "The works?"

"They have to ask for help," said Crawford with a shrug. "Just in case, how many men can we put in the air, and how soon?"

Stemple rapped out, "The squads on duty are full strength. That's fifty men in ten minutes. A hundred more from the nearest feeder base, one hour. Forty from the outer base, two hours."

"Make quite a show, wouldn't it?" asked Crawford contentedly. But the minutes dragged by and there was no word from the hard-pressed firefighters of Idaho. "No fire boss likes to admit he's licked," the Air Service Chief added finally.

"Message to our region going through now," said Gray in his emotionless way. "Idaho's asking for help."

Crawford sprang out of his chair. "Alert the outfit," he roared.

Stemple turned toward the entrance to the bunk room. But it was empty, and two pairs of feet were pounding down the hallway.

SIXTEEN

THE PLANE flew with the angry whine of maximum power. It was a high-speed commercial transport, converted to aerial firefighting by ripping out all the luxurious fittings. Four squads of smokejumpers were ranged against the duralumin walls of the cabin, a hobgoblin array in their armored jumpsuits. They sat motionless and quiet as statues. In the first place, they were packed in too tightly to do any moving around. In the second, they had been through the same routine too often to waste any energy before jumping. There would be plenty to see and do when they got to their destination.

The surest way to make one of the smokejumpers laugh was to show him a newspaper story telling how daring and romantic he was. As their jumpsuits proved—stained, scuffed and often mended—all the romance had been knocked out of them long ago. They were professionals, doing a hard, dirty and dangerous job. If there was always the unforgettable thrill of the jump, there was always too the long walk back, lugging sixty pounds of equipment. So they stretched out in the plane as far as the fire packs piled along the center aisle would let them, and relaxed.

Up near the door to the pilot's compartment, Stemple, Parker and the four squad leaders had their heads together. Stemple was saying, "We're going into this sort of blind. No maps. Too much smoke to look it over from the air. But it won't matter; we're going in on it as an outfit."

"Crawford's dream comes true," remarked Jim. "How many is he putting in?"

"Every man he can outfit with a chute, minus the twelve that are down in our own area. Close to two hundred."

The squad leaders looked at each other and whistled. Stemple continued, "This deal is a bunch of lightning fires all in an area about two miles square. The ground crews have been trying to fight each fire separately. Don't asked me who dreamed that up, when it took two days to get the first crew in there. It's the boss's fire now. He's going to fight it on the perimeter and let it burn out inside."

"The boss coming on it himself?" asked one of the squad leaders.

Stemple smiled briefly. "He was in a jump suit and buckling up his harness when the Old Man came and told him nothing doing."

"The Regional Forester? What was he doing out at the base?"

"Oh, this is big stuff, the first massed use of smokejumpers. Crawford's been waiting all season for it. And now he has to run the party by radio from Midvale. When I left he was so mad he couldn't talk."

"Well, how about letting those fires join up inside the perimeter. Whole thing's liable to blow up, isn't it?"

"Sure. That's a chance we have to take. The weatherman is giving us a reasonable break: higher humidity and light wind for the next couple of days. We're taking the northwest sector. We'll jump by squads and tackle the hottest spots. The others'll start coming over in an hour and will fill in the gaps."

The door to the pilot's compartment had been removed along with the other trimmings of a passenger ship. Now the copilot got Stemple's attention simply by reaching out and hammering on his parachute pack. Stemple turned and took a yellow message form from him. For several moments the smokejumper foreman studied it. Across his face passed all the emotions of a man meeting a sudden emergency, scrapping at a blow one carefully prepared plan and instantly making a new one.

Finally he held the message out so that the others could read it all at once. It said:

> Patrol reports private ship making forced landing in fire area. Investigate. Parker lead rescue party.
>
> Crawford

A rescue mission was no novelty to the smokejumpers. All over the northwest their parachutes were becoming a symbol of help to the lost, sick and injured. But a plane crash in the middle of a forest fire was something new. Stemple conferred briefly with the pilot.

When he came back he said, "We'll be there in a few minutes. We'll drag the burn and see if we can spot the wreck. Lefty, pick your crew."

Since his fight with Hank there had been a change in Lefty Parker, though not on the surface. Outwardly he was his arrogant, impatient self. The change showed mostly in the way other people treated him: first-year jumpers now asked his advice —and got a civil answer instead of a sneer; Stemple called him by his first name; Crawford even assigned him as the leader of a rescue party. If he had been there to hear what followed, Crawford would have smiled approval of this slightly different Parker.

He asked, "Can I have anyone I want?"

"I reckon," replied John Stemple.

"O.K. I'll take Hank, Jim and Charley Bear Dance."

"Particular, aren't you?" grinned Stemple. "All right, you three, notify your alternate squad leaders and get ready to flit."

The explanations and arrangements were quickly made. An almost complete change in plan and leadership was nothing to upset a smokejumper crew. Looking out the cabin window when they were finished, Hank and Jim could see an enormous cloud of blue smoke looming up ahead. Hanging above the earth, fed constantly by the upward rush of vapor from the many fires, it was an awe-inspiring sight even to the smokejumpers.

"Trust Lefty to grab us for this rodeo," growled Jim.

Hank laughed at him. "Your heart'd break if he didn't."

The plane flew directly into the cloud, and the acrid sting of smoke immediately irritated their eyes and nostrils. Inside, the cloud was not as dense as it appeared from a distance. They could see the jumble of mountains and canyons unrolling below, all mantled in the somber green of the doomed forest.

Quickly they located the scene of the crash. From a tiny clearing near the top of a low, dome-shaped mountain rose a column of smoke of a different kind. It was black and oily and shot with orange flashes. The smokejumper plane hardly had to change course to pass over it. Inside, the rescue party cleared for the take-off.

Hank and Jim removed the cabin door entirely and set it to one side in its clamps. Parker and

Charley hustled up two fire packs. Each of these, topped by its cargo chute and streamers, contained tools, emergency rations, and a parachutist's radio well padded with sleeping bags.

Stemple moved to the spotter's position. Taking his station by the open door, he prepared to drop the pilot chute. This was a tiny canopy no larger than a handkerchief, weighted with a small sandbag. It was designed to duplicate the descent of a smoke-jumper. By dropping it in advance, the spotter could judge wind direction and force and so choose the plane's line of approach and the release point for the parachutists.

As the plane leveled off, Stemple pointed to the smoke column climbing straight from the wrecked plane. Above the banshee howl of wind in the door-way he shouted, "No wind. Want to save time and go down without the pilot chute?"

Parker's helmet nodded agreement.

The copilot had swung round in his seat now and was watching Stemple. With hand signals Stemple motioned right or left as the plane drifted over the target. The copilot relayed these signals to the pilot.

Parker had edged the fire packs right into the doorway. He stood behind them, grasping the handholds on either side of the oval frame. Behind him in close single file were Charley, Jim and Hank. From a steel rod in the roof, the looping band of the static cord ran down to the chute pack of each. Stemple jerked them one after the other to make sure they were properly hooked.

Now his hand hovered motionless; the plane flew straight and steady. Then the spotter made a downward chopping motion with his hand. Instantly the engine rumble died away and the plane lost speed. It drifted forward. The figures at the door were tensely poised, the four helmeted heads craning toward the earth.

Release came almost casually. Stemple tapped Parker on the shoulder. With a heave of his knees Parker pushed out the fire packs. They fell away, trailing their orange streamers. Stemple tapped him again, and in one continuous rush the smokejumpers lunged into space. Four reports, so close together that they overlapped, hammered the plane's metal hide. Four white canopies materialized in mid air.

Like an anxious parent the ship circled down with the drifting chutes. So close together that their collapsing canopies made a single white blotch on the ground, the smokejumpers landed. One of them looked up and waved as the plane churned the smoky air above them.

"That, my friends, is chute handling," said Stemple quietly.

✿ SEVENTEEN ✿

ＯＲＤＩＮＡＲＩＬＹ the Air Service communications center was a place reserved for Ben Gray, the dispatcher, with his battery of radios and telephones and his sheaves of maps. Occasionally Stemple or Crawford might come in for a few minutes to read the reports or listen to the loudspeaker telling the course of some invisible battle against a fire. Now and then a squad leader would exercise his privilege of wisecracking with the dispatcher or studying a map with professional interest.

That today he had an unusually large and distinguished audience disturbed Gray not a bit. He could listen to a couple of radio transmissions and a telephone call at the same time and keep them sorted out. It took more than the Regional Forester, the Air Service Chief and two important-looking strangers to upset him.

A deep, heavy rumble overhead made him raise his eyes momentarily.

"There they go," said Crawford. He looked pleadingly at the Regional Forester.

"For the last time, no," replied Manley in his mild voice. "All you're after is to crack a chute yourself. You're jump-happy."

"Any word about my boy and Katy? Anything at all?" The despairing croak was hardly recognizable as the voice of Senator Donahue.

Crawford looked at the pleading eyes and sagging shoulders. For this tortured man he felt only sympathy, in spite of their past differences. "Too soon," he explained. "They're just about coming over the fire area now. They'll have to hunt. Not too easy in the smoke."

It was Senator Winton, the fourth member of the party, who had brought Donahue to the communications center. Familiar with the ways and methods of the Forest Service, he had known where to go the moment the news flash came that Senator Donahue's son and granddaughter were crash-landing in the middle of a forest fire. If he was thinking that his own son was about to jump into that same fire under a frail canopy of nylon, he kept it to himself.

With one hand at the dials and the other pressing an earphone to his head, Ben Gray tuned a radio delicately. "This is about the limit of his range, but there he is," said the dispatcher. He pulled the jack of his earphone out of the panel and a faraway voice whispered:

"—to Midvale. Calling Midvale. Relay from Parker. He reports pilot and passenger safe. Do you read me, Midvale? Over."

"Midvale back. Read you O.K. Go ahead."

"Parker reports he and one man going after pilot who left crash to look for help. Other two men taking passenger out of fire area. I am standing by for further contact. Stemple reports on his sector. All squads down and organized. He says to hurry those reinforcements. Clear and standing by."

"Thank God," said Donahue. "How long before they're out of there? Why doesn't that man Parker report more often?" The normal hue was coming back into the senator's face and the organ tone to his voice.

Crawford looked annoyed and Manley spoke quickly. "He can't very well trail your son, dodge forest fires and work a radio all at the same time. It may be several hours before we hear from him again."

"And those two with my granddaughter. Are you sure they're competent?" The senator had recovered completely.

There was lightning in Crawford's eyes, but Senator Winton managed to forestall the flash and the Air Service Chief replied quietly, "Just the best in the world. My two top squad leaders."

An hour dragged by, long as only an hour can be for people who must wait. The drama of the struggle taking place out there beyond sight came to them in clipped radio transmissions. Another fifty smokejumpers were down and on the fire line. Fifty more were spilling out of their planes. Somehow the feeling of the excitement, even the picture of it reached across the miles and through the background of static. The planes sailing over the fire, the pilot chutes going down. Then the fire packs with fluttering streamers. Finally the jumpers, maneuvering warily in the vicious air currents around the fires.

Once the static cleared momentarily, and they actually heard Stemple on his powerful foreman's set directing the last flight of transports. Unable to sit still, Crawford paced the room like a tiger. *His* dream, *his* planning, *his* men making the dream come true. And he was three hundred miles away!

At last the ghostly voice spoke again: "Calling Midvale. Relay from Parker. He has found the pilot, Donahue. They are through the fire. He will go to Lost Lake airfield. Requests pickup by patrol plane. Pilot is injured."

There was a short flurry of radio messages back and forth as the pickup was arranged. And then the play was over for one actor. Senator Donahue's son was winging toward a Midvale hospital.

"Still no word about my little Katy," muttered Donahue. "What in the world are those fellows doing?"

"They're trying to get out of a tighter squeeze than you ever saw," flamed Crawford. He went to his map of the fire area and began to study it. Then he spoke to himself out loud as he strove to project his mind into the minds of the smokejumpers:

"They don't have maps . . . don't know the country . . . They'll look for the side where the fires are thinnest . . . south. But that way they won't meet any ground crews . . . and they're heading for the worst mass of country in North America, the Whitetail Marsh and the old 1910 burn . . . Ben." On the last word his voice cut like a knife. "Send this message to the relay plane. He's to call the rescue party every fifteen minutes and tell them not to go south. Got that? *Don't go south!*"

✤ EIGHTEEN ✤

ALTHOUGH last out of the plane, Hank had been the first to land. Heavier than the others, his rate of descent was faster than theirs. Hands tense on the guide lines, he watched the earth rush up at him. It was always like that. No sensation of falling. The earth was moving, not he. It never failed to give him a queer burning sensation in the pit of his stomach, a moment of panic. With Jim, he knew from countless bull sessions, it was just the opposite. Jim had a mortal fear of leaving the plane, a fear he would have died rather than confess to anyone but Hank.

The ground was very close now. Hank began to work his guide lines delicately, maneuvering his chute toward a grassy spot, free of boulders. A smokejumper had to be prepared to land on anything from the top of a hundred-foot spruce to a rock slide. But he had no objection to smooth footing if he could find it.

Through the latticework of his helmet he caught glimpses of the burning plane. Then he saw something that almost caused him to make a fatal mistake. A short distance from the plane he spotted a small figure lying on the ground, probably that of a child.

For a moment Hank forgot that making a parachute landing calls for absolute concentration. He began to oscillate violently, swinging from side to side under his canopy like a huge pendulum. But his training and the lightning reflexes of a boxer saved him. He jerked one guide line so savagely that the steering slot cracked like a whip. His flailing body hung perpendicular again, and at that instant his boots hit the earth. With arms pressed close to his ribs, Hank made the forward half-roll, half-somersault the smokejumper uses to absorb the landing shock.

He rose to his feet again and struck the quick-release buckle with his clenched fist. The complicated pattern of his jumping harness fell away, taking the emergency chute pack on his chest with it. Hank started running toward the plane before his canopy had time to settle. As he ran he heard close by the characteristic thud and grunt of another smokejumper's landing.

The small figure near the smoking wreckage sat up as Hank approached. He saw to his amazement that it was a little girl. She stared at him with enormous black eyes and shrank back.

Instantly Hank realized what was the matter. He tore off his helmet, revealing his unruly thatch of hair and an unmistakably friendly grin.

"I didn't mean to scare you, honey," he said, dropping to his knees beside her. "Are you all right?"

The child replied, "I'm all right now. I didn't know what you were at first. You looked awful."

One by one the other smokejumpers ran up, Jim, Parker and finally Charley Bear Dance. If anyone had been there to see it, they made a strange picture, the enormous smokejumpers gathered round the little girl like demon soldiers protecting a fairy queen. On all sides of them was desolation, the heat-tortured framework of the plane, the black skeletons of burned trees and the smoke. The child looked up at them and smiled.

"What happened?" asked Parker.

"Engine conked," she answered professionally. "My daddy dead-sticked her into this clearing. He's the greatest flyer in the world."

"He must be," agreed Parker, "to get in here with a dead engine. But where is he?"

"He went to get help."

Gloomily Parker looked at the encircling smoke. Here on the ground it was much thicker than aloft. It stung the eyes and hurt in the lungs. Seen through it, the shape of everything was distorted and unreal.

"Which way did he go, honey?" prompted Hank.

Without hesitation the girl pointed north. "He said where there's a forest fire there are sure to be firefighters."

"Not bad reasoning," commented Jim.

"If he doesn't walk into an explosion," added Parker under his breath. "Some of these fires are about ready to blow up." He raised his voice,

"Charley and I'll go after the pilot. Hank, you and Jim take the girl and get her out of here. Abandon all your equipment except what you need for traveling and your radio. This looks like a good place to get away from."

They could see for themselves that the smoke was getting thicker and could feel the harsh blast of heat flowing over the clearing.

"Any ideas which way to go?" asked Jim.

"Take your pick," retorted Parker grimly. "We've got no maps. Only don't go north. Fires're thickest there." He and Charley were already tearing open one of the fire packs. They discarded everything in it but the emergency rations, first-aid kits, the radio and an axe apiece.

Parker opened the tiny set and said, "Parker to Stemple, Parker to Stemple, over."

Instantly he got a reply from the plane hovering unseen in the smoke.

"Parker to Stemple," continued the leader. "We're at the wreck. Pilot and passenger O.K. Pilot left to look for help. Charley and I going after him. Dade and Winton taking passenger out of fire area. Relay to base. Over."

"Got you, Lefty," came Stemple's voice. "Will do. Standing by."

"Good luck, you guys," said Parker. "Be seeing you." He and Charley disappeared into the haze.

Jim, pawing over the contents of their fire pack, said, "You know, we're liable to be out overnight. The kid will freeze. We'd better take one of the parachutes. We can all sleep in that."

Hank nodded agreement. He was struggling out of the stiff embrace of his jumpsuit.

"Better leave that on a while," remarked Jim with a significant glance at the boiling smoke. "Might need it." He rolled their rations and radio up in his parachute and strapped the bundle to one of the pack boards.

The child still sat where they had found her. Hank said, "Time to move, honey. Want to take my hand?"

Gravely she replied, "Thanks, but I can't walk. My ankles are sprained. That's why my daddy told me to stay here."

Hank felt a sudden constriction in his throat and unaccountably his eyes blurred. He walked a little to one side with Jim.

"Better bandage her up a little," said the latter. "I'll scout around and see if I can pick a way out of this coke oven. And don't start blubbering."

"She's got so much nerve," retorted Hank defensively. "Not a squawk out of her, and there she's been sitting all this time with two sprained ankles."

"Itsy-bitsy, widgy-squidgy," jeered Jim, and sprang out of range.

Breaking open a first-aid kit, Hank returned to the little girl. Sprained ankles were nothing new to a smokejumper. He understood just how to bandage her feet so that her ankles were cushioned and protected.

"Tell me if I'm hurting you," he said. "What's your name, anyway?"

"My name's Katy. How can I go anywhere if I can't walk? And what about Daddy? He said to stay here."

Hank explained, "You can't do that. It's going to be on fire in a few minutes. Don't worry about your dad. My two side-kicks will take care of him. And you're going to ride on my shoulders. I'm Hank. Pleased to meet you, Katy."

"Pleased to meet you, Hank." They shook hands formally.

"And my partner's name is Jim." Hank was in a fever to be off. He could read fire signs too well not to know that in a very short time this clearing would be the center of an inferno. But he went on calmly, "Where were you headed for, Katy, when your engine conked?"

"To see my granddaddy," replied the girl. "I had on a new dress too," she added sorrowfully.

It looked anything but new now. The thin, gay-colored fabric was torn and smudged. A ribbon was still in her hair, but the hair itself was full of dust and twigs and grass.

Hank consoled her, "Never mind. I bet when your granddaddy sees you he'll buy you a whole box full of dresses."

The outlandish figure of Jim Dade came out of the smoke. "All set?" he asked briskly.

"All set." Hank lifted Katy to his shoulders. "What'd you find out?"

"Oh, we can get through," replied Jim with a confidence in his voice that did not quite match the tense look around his eyes. "We'll have to go through one burn."

Hank looked at him, knowing what those simple words "through a burn" might mean. "Maybe we ought to radio a report to the plane," he suggested.

"Time enough for that when we get out and hook up with a crew. Let's get going," retorted Jim impatiently.

He led off into the bluish gloom, and Hank's long legs carried him and Katy after. "Which way're we headed?" he asked.

"Who cares, without a map?" Jim called over his shoulder. "But since you ask it's—south."

✦ NINETEEN ✦

〰〰〰〰〰〰〰〰〰〰〰〰〰〰〰

"YOU MEAN we're lost?" asked Katy, looking at Hank with solemn eyes.

"Not lost, exactly," replied the big smokejumper. He was stretched flat on his back on a grassy bank and looked a little less gigantic now that he had got rid of his bulky jumpsuit. "We just don't know where we are."

Behind them, dim in the smoke, rose a low but very steep range of mountains. In front of them and to either side stretched the level green-and-silver expanse of an alpine marsh. Its boundaries were lost in the bluish fire haze. There was no sign that any human being had ever before set foot in the region. The pungent odor of wood smoke hid the smell of grass and water. They could hear only the distracted crying of a mother duck hustling her brood away from the invaders.

"Well, it sounds like lost to me," insisted Katy.

Hank grinned at her. "Look at it this way. The deal came up so suddenly that they couldn't get maps to us. We didn't even have time for a look at the country from the air. But nobody's really lost in the mountains until he loses his nerve. We know that water flows downhill, that springs run into creeks and creeks into rivers and that somewhere close to water we'll find a house or a road or a trail."

Katy remarked, "We've been following this water a long time and it doesn't seem to be flowing anywhere. But"—and a smile lit her small face—"if you say so, we aren't lost. When's Jim coming back?"

They heard the missing smokejumper before they could see him through the stinging fog. He was splashing along in the water, which was much faster and easier than going through the dense willows on shore. He was talking to himself, in Jim a sure sign of discouragement. "Smokejumpers," he was muttering with infinite scorn. "Toss 'em out of a plane, leave 'em alone and they'll come home, wagging their chutes behind them. Phooey!"

He squelched up onto the bank and sat down

beside Katy. Immediately he pulled off his boots and wrung out his socks. His feet were white and wrinkled from long soaking, and he began to massage them. A firefighter, no less than a soldier, is only as good as his feet.

"Let me," said Katy. "You rest." She scrambled over, pulled his feet into her lap, and began to rub industriously.

Hank enjoyed the odd parade of emotions across Jim's face: surprise, unbelief, consternation and finally pleasure. There had been little kindness in Jim Dade's life, and he was suspicious of it. But he was learning.

In a single day this seven-year-old girl had won over the two smokejumpers completely. It could so easily have been different. At first she just represented a job dumped into their laps, and a difficult one at that. She was helpless, unused to the forest and not even dressed for wilderness hardships. She might get sick; she was a mouth to feed. Most serious of all, she was sixty or seventy pounds of weight that could not be abandoned in an emergency like a parachute. Getting her safely out of the mountains was a task to make even a smokejumper scratch his head.

But by a thousand little acts of cheerfulness and good sense the child had shown her bravery. A smokejumper takes courage as a matter of course. He sees it in action every day. But he seldom sees it wrapped up in so small a package.

When the three had left the scene of the plane crash, they were completely surrounded by the fire. For anyone but trained foresters that would have ended the story. Hank and Jim, however, knew better than to let the flames catch them inside their ravenous circle. They resorted to the veteran fire-fighter's last trick. Picking the moment and the spot, they broke through. On Hank's shoulders Katy had run the flaming gantlet with trees exploding into mighty torches all around her, under a rain of red-hot cinders, in strangling gas and blinding smoke. But though tears streaked her sooty face, she had never cried out loud.

Moving as carefully as he could, Hank now and then knocked her bandaged ankles against a tree. But beyond a whimper quickly stifled, she never complained.

Even the tough smokejumpers had grown tired. Outwitting the fire, they had traveled steadily south all the rest of the day and well into the night. They knew only too well how swiftly a fire can turn in its tracks and take up the pursuit.

They had hoped any minute to meet one of the ground crews with food and maps, perhaps even horses. Instead they had found this endless marsh. For hours they had splashed along its brush-choked shores, looking for the outlet. But if Katy had been hungry and exhausted, she never said so.

Hank had surrendered instantly to the child. His progress through the marsh with her on his shoulders was a continuous round of teasing and non-sense. Jim watched them with an expression that said no one was going to catch *him* going soft. But when Hank had suddenly found the little girl top-pling off his shoulders, it was Jim who took up the sleeping figure and carried her for miles, cradled in his arms.

"Itsy-bitsy, widgy-squidgy," Hank had whispered, getting his revenge at last. But Jim only blinked at him, expressionless as an owl.

"I suppose it was the same old jabber-jabber, yak-kity-yak all the time I was gone," grunted Jim when his feet were pink and smooth again, thanks to Katy's work. "I don't suppose you jokers even heard the plane that's been circling us for the last hour. Of course he's only trying to make a radio contact."

Hank started up guiltily. Now he could hear the faint drone, muffled by smoke. Now near, now far, the unseen ship buzzed overhead. There was a message in its very persistence. Hank flipped the "receive" switch of their tiny radio-telephone. But no answering hum of static came from it. When he moved the switch over to "transmit," there was no power hum.

Every fifteen minutes the plane drove its message earthward: "Message from Crawford to Dade and Winton. Don't go south. Dade and Winton, don't go south. Do you read me, Dade and Winton? Don't go south." But through the smoke the pilot could not see the figures in the swamp below him.

Grimy, red-eyed fire foremen held up their own urgent messages to leave the channel clear. Amateur radio operators hundreds of miles away picked it up and puzzled over its meaning. Stemple, who could read Crawford's mind at any range, flashed a request from the fire line for permission to lead a search party.

He got back a terse, "Request denied. Mind your own business." With Crawford the red enemy would always come first.

In the faraway communications center, the search plane reported "no contact" hour after hour. "I demand that you stop frittering away time in this idiotic manner and organize rescue parties," shouted Senator Donahue. His face was mottled with rage and anxiety.

"Ten thousand woodsmen could probably do the job, if you know where to find them and how to transport them," retorted Crawford.

"Your far-famed smokejumpers would do as a start," fumed the senator.

Neither the Regional Forester nor Senator Winton was present this time to intervene. The two men faced each other. One was an important political figure, long used to power and to having his own way. The other was the first woodsman and fire-fighter of the northwest. Anyone from Regional Forester Manley to the newest first-year man could have told Donahue, however, that absolutely no one can interfere with a fire boss, especially Air Service Chief Crawford, in the midst of combat.

Here at the center of his communications web, Crawford was a prisoner of radios and telephones. His nerves were stretched tight as violin strings to catch every shade of meaning in the brief messages that poured in. Longing in every fiber to be on the fire line, in the dust and smoke and heat, he had to stay and hold in his fingers all the threads of manpower, transportation, food and equipment. On his shoulders rested the murderous weight of planning, of knowing that his decisions were final and that upon them depended the safety of millions of dollars worth of timber, grass and water—and the lives of men.

Crawford had seldom raised his voice, and did not then. But he propelled his words like bullets. "If it weren't for my far-famed smokejumpers, you wouldn't know what happened to either your son or granddaughter. As it is, one of them is already safe, here in this room. Two hundred men could do no more for the girl than those two smokejumpers. I can give you a personal guarantee that if she doesn't get out, they won't either. Now I'll give you a choice. Either stop meddling or get out. This is no debating society."

Donahue's face turned white. But before he could find his voice, a third person spoke. In a lean, youthful way he resembled the senator. His face was liberally criss-crossed with adhesive tape, and one arm hung in a sling. He wore the silver wings of an army pilot. "He's right, Dad," said the senator's son. "If those two are anything like the pair that came after me, Katy couldn't be safer."

"She'd better be safe," choked the senator. "Because if she isn't, I'll nail the hide of a forester to every tree between here and Washington."

✿ TWENTY ✿

ON THE EDGE of the Whitetail Marsh, Jim Dade shook a fist at the invisible plane still humming above the smoke, and yelled, "So I fell into a pothole in this lousy bog and got the radio full of water. Want to make something of it?"

Katy looked at him with alarm, but Hank understood that Jim was merely disgusted with himself. Hank said, "I don't see where it makes much difference. What can the guy up there tell us? He can't see anything. For that matter, what could we tell him? We're in a swamp. So what?"

Without answering, Jim reached for his boots. He turned his back so that Hank wouldn't see the one that was coming apart. Baked during the dash through the fire, then water-soaked for hours, even the select leather of smokejumper boots began to deteriorate.

"You might as well have it right between the eyes," he said finally. "We've been all the way round this bog, and it doesn't have any outlet."

"*All* the way round?" echoed Hank.

"Yep. I found the ration box where we ate this morning about half a mile from here."

Hank laughed ruefully, "Some woodsmen we turned out to be, walking in a circle like dudes."

"No visibility, no landmarks, no map," Jim pointed out. "But we should have smelled that there was no outlet. We've seen enough of these alpine ponds that drain underground."

"Is it very bad?" Katy looked anxiously from one of her protectors to the other.

"Not bad at all," replied Hank hastily. "Just aggravating. We've wasted the best part of a day."

But he and Jim knew that it was very bad. Their long disappearance would cause worry and heartache. Crawford might strip his fire lines of men to look for them. Most of all, they dreaded the consequences for Katy. Already the child had gone through enough pain and hardship to put her in a hospital. How much more could she stand?

There were angles to this affair not covered even in the Smokechaser's Bible. There had been no time for standard preparations. Ordinarily a chutist would descend on his wilderness target fully supplied with maps and instructions. He would know in which direction and how far off lay the nearest food cache, shelter, road, trail, telephone or radio and airfield. With his own radio he could call for help. If he went unreported too long, rescue crews would know exactly where to look for him.

From the start all this protection and support had been denied Hank and Jim. They had been thrown on a moment's notice into a completely strange wilderness. An accident had robbed them of their means of communication. Smoke hid them from search planes. And as Crawford had tried to explain to Donahue, without knowing their location and route, ten thousand men could comb the mountains without finding their trail.

By themselves, the smokejumpers would have had no worries. They might be lost by any definition except a forester's but, wilderness trained and toughened, they could feel perfectly safe even if it took them a week to find their way out. It was Katy who tipped the balance against them.

Jim finished lacing his boots and said, "Well, what'll we try next?"

"How about finding ourselves another watercourse?" suggested Hank.

Jim nodded agreement. "Might as well keep on south, too. Quickest way to get shut of this bog hole."

Thus, as Crawford had foreseen and tried vainly to prevent, they exchanged the gateless maze of the swamp for a worse puzzle. By doing everything a well-trained woodsman should, they were getting themselves into a still worse situation.

The mountains bordering the marsh on the south were low but exceedingly steep, actually mere heaps of shattered rock. The first part of the climb was over fields of shale where every step loosed a clattering avalanche. Struggling through that, they came to larger and larger rocks until at last they scrambled over boulders as big as houses. Often Hank, standing on tiptoe with Katy balanced in his arms, could just barely hoist her to Jim on the ledge above. It was slow and tiring work. It was also dangerous.

Jim muttered a "glad that's over" when at last they reached the summit.

From the ridge they hopefully surveyed the new territory. Below them the mountainside fell away into a deep canyon. At its bottom they could make out the polished gleam of wet rock and occasional plumes of spray. That was exactly what they wanted, a stream that definitely went somewhere.

But in the same glance they saw something else that made them look quickly at each other and as quickly away again. There is no sight in the world more forbidding than the desolation left by a great forest fire.

What confronted them was an old burn. They could tell its age from the young growth struggling up through the mat of fallen logs. And it was immense. Ridge beyond ridge and canyon behind canyon, they saw it as the wind momentarily blew aside the veil of smoke. It had been a climax forest, the trees standing close and straight and tall. From lordly elk to fierce-eyed weasel the wilderness tribes had found food and shelter there. Now only a creature that crawled or flew could find a path through the gigantic jackstraw tangle of logs and brush.

Most of the great trees had fallen one upon the other, every which way. But even after almost forty years, some of them still stood. With an odd regularity their naked, silvery trunks and distorted arms brooded over the vanquished forest like grave markers over the bodies of the slain.

"What—happened?" asked Katy in a small voice. Wilderness-wise or not, no one could mistake catastrophe on such a scale.

"1910," replied Jim simply.

To any forester that date explained everything. It was the year when twenty-two million acres went up in flame and smoke and the Forest Service was born. For some reason Hank thought of Senator Donahue and his grudge and wished that the senator could be present. The Forest Service was the only barrier against destruction such as this in any year.

With a shrug Jim set his foot on the bole of a fallen log and catwalked along it. There was no turning back now, and no way to go ahead except along the zigzag pathway of logs. Sometimes Jim led the nightmare journey twenty feet above the ground. His axe was continually at work lopping off brush and dead branches. Hank followed along the aerial highway he built, Katy balanced on his shoulders. He moved sure-footed but with painful deliberation. A fall here could only mean injury.

Breaking trail, Jim set a murderous pace. Without exchanging a word, he and Hank knew that they must get out of the labyrinth before darkness forced them to halt. Though the burn looked as peaceful as a cemetery, it was full of menace to the travelers. It was a heap of tinder reckoned in square miles, ready to explode from a wind-borne cinder or a spark of lightning. Most of the dead standing trees were merely balanced on their decayed roots, ready to topple at a breath of wind. It was actually a desert, without water, without food, without shelter.

Sometimes Jim was close ahead, hacking through buck brush and scrub pine. More often he was out of sight, scouting the best path for Hank and his awkward burden. Always he left behind a marked and cleared trail.

After one disappearance, longer than the others, Hank saw that Jim had wrapped his left foot in a piece of nylon. Katy apparently didn't notice, and there was no reason to frighten her. Jim could have done it for many reasons. He might have fallen and hurt his ankle. Balanced precariously on a log, it is only too easy to drive an axe into flesh and bone instead of wood. Jim could still travel, though he was limping, which was all that mattered at the moment.

"Good news, folks," said Jim. "We're almost out of the burn. There's an up-canyon breeze lifting the smoke. And there's a lake. I mean the genuine article, no swamp."

"I go for that breeze," said Hank. Under the constant irritation of the blue haze they all coughed and cried continually. But Hank's eyes had been extra-sensitive ever since the time he pulled Jim out of the flames the year before. In forester language, he had been "smoked up."

An alpine lake. That meant much to a forester. It meant protection from any fire that overtook them. It meant rest and shelter in the live timber hugging its shores. It meant food. Quite possibly it meant a trail or even a road.

Just as Jim had said, the smoke was lifting. Soon they made out the lake, blue-black and so utterly still that it was hard to tell where trees ended and reflections began.

"It's beautiful," cried the girl. "Do you suppose it has a name?"

"Probably not," replied Jim. "Anyway, we found it, so we'll just name it ourselves. Lake—Lake Katy."

"Thanks very much," said the little girl demurely. "I always wanted a lake of my own. Giddyap, Hank. I want to see my lake close up."

In this light-hearted manner they ended the second twenty-four hours of their journey out of danger. Actually it was dark before they gained the refuge. They had to fight through a final mile of the burn and then a mile of virgin forest, which was easy going only by comparison with the previous part of their trek.

They camped in a stand of huge old firs where the interlaced branches made a sort of room, windproof and rainproof. The roots of the trees had twisted themselves into natural armchairs padded with a mat of needles inches thick. While Jim scraped a hole in it down to bare earth and lined it with rock for a fireplace, Hank scurried around in the gloom dragging in every dry log and branch he could find. Soon the ruddy glow of their campfire held the darkness and the night chill at arm's length.

They washed the sting of smoke out of their eyes and throats with icy lake water. Then, ceremoniously, they divided the last of their food. No need to save it now. Hank, flourishing a bedraggled Royal Coachman fly, had promised them trout for breakfast. At that, the portions were meager: a mouthful of canned meat, a bit of chocolate and a handful of cracker crumbs apiece.

Smokejumpers travel light, expecting to go hungry. What food Hank and Jim had they had lavished on the little girl, until she caught them at it. After that she wouldn't touch a morsel until they had eaten their share. The lake, with its promise of generous rations, was a real godsend, the only piece of good fortune they'd had.

"Time for young ladies with lakes named after them to hit the hay," said Hank when the last crumb was gone.

He bundled Katy up in the parachute and put her down out of range of flying sparks. For several minutes there was no sound except for the popping of the fire and the deep, even breathing of the child.

"All right," said Hank then, "what's the matter with your foot?"

"I'm ashamed to tell you," growled Jim. "When I saw the lake I got so hepped up I jumped off a log and ran right through a patch of devil's club. Wouldn't have been so bad except my boot picked that time to fall apart."

Every woodsman of the northwest dreads devil's club, a plant quilled like a porcupine. "Nice," said Hank. "Get all the stickers out?"

Jim shook his head. "Most of them broke off." He didn't mention the agony of trying to pull those barbed and poisoned spines, or of walking on the buried points.

"Quite a mess we're in, isn't it?" remarked Hank as casually as if he had said it was a nice day.

"Yeah," agreed Jim. "You blind yet?" His tone was just as flat as Hank's.

"Not quite. I can still see the fire." By tensing every muscle Hank kept his voice steady. He had seen smoke blindness before, had even experienced a touch of it himself. He knew it wasn't permanent, but no man could feel the light going out of his eyes without a rush of panic. The pain, as if a hand-ful of sand were packed under each eyelid, was actually welcome. It kept him from thinking about anything else.

From the sound of Jim's movements Hank knew when he hobbled round the fire and sat beside him. Jim didn't take hold of him or say a word, just sat there with his shoulder touching Hank's. Gradually the terror subsided, the insane desire to run and scream.

"If I had your feet or you had my lamps, we'd be a smokejumper," said Jim eventually.

And Hank managed to laugh.

✣ TWENTY-ONE ✣

ON THE SHORE of Lake Katy there was a scene familiar to any camper. A fire burned brightly inside a stone fireplace. Beside it a tousle-headed giant was peeling willow wands, sharpening them into skewers. A little girl watched with absorbed interest.

At first glance it was a peaceful, happy scene. Smoke made a canopy that hid the sky, but the sun had burned a brassy hole in it. A gentle canyon breeze swept the poisonous odor of the fog away from the lake. Not far away Jim Dade was perched on a rock overhanging the water. With a willow pole, a cord made by tying together threads from a parachute shroud line and Hank's Royal Coachman, he was fishing.

At second glance the picture lacked something. There was no food being cooked, no bubbling coffee pot, no sizzling pan, no odor of bacon or fragrance of hotcakes. The pair by the fire were much too dirty and haggard for campers. They looked like refugees.

Hank laid down the skewers and put his knife back in its scabbard. He said, "That takes care of the cooking tools. Guess I'll go soak the eyes again."

He held out his hand and Katy took it. Carefully she led him down to the lake where he splashed the healing water into his face.

"How many fish has Jim caught?" Hank turned as if trying to see for himself. But his puffy eyelids were swollen shut, and an endless procession of tears oozed down his cheeks.

"I—I don't think he's caught any," replied Katy unhappily.

"Barren lake. Isn't that just our luck?" Nothing in Hank's voice told the little girl that this was the worst blow of all. But sensitive nerves warned her that in some way more important than a missed breakfast, the lake had failed them.

"C'mon Jim, give it up," called Hank. "If there were any fish in this pothole you'd have a dozen by now."

"You mustn't call my lake a pothole," reproved Katy, but she couldn't get much spirit into it. Nothing seemed to matter much any more. She wasn't even hungry, just tired and sleepy. Sometimes when she spoke her tongue tripped over the simplest words, or she'd forget what she had wanted to say.

In a burst of temper, Jim threw his rod into the brush. He had fashioned a crutch out of a small aspen and came hobbling back to them on it, putting the least possible weight on the ball of nylon that covered his foot. It was swollen now to twice normal size and horribly painful.

There was no point in trying to deceive Katy any more. The two smokejumpers discussed their problem as if she were a jumper herself. Actually she was never more than half awake now and it mattered little what they said.

"Any chance of making a smoke signal?" asked Hank. "A good smudge would bring a patrol plane or a smokechaser in a hurry."

Dade replied, "No good. Too much fog in the air already."

There was silence while in their minds the two smokejumpers went back over their trail trying to puzzle out what it was they had done to get into this plight. With a shock, they realized that they had done nothing wrong. Everything they had done had been good woodscraft. Alone, they would never have run from the fire. They'd have skirted its edges, looking for a ground crew. But with Katy to look after they couldn't take a chance on getting trapped a second time. Their only choice was to retreat. With every bit of skill and determination they possessed they had fought to get Katy out of the wilderness. And everything had gone wrong. It was as if the wilderness had turned against them.

Even now, crippled, blind, exhausted and starving, the plight of the smokejumpers wasn't too serious. In a day or so Hank would regain enough eyesight to travel. The spines in Dade's foot would fester and come out by themselves. A little starvation wouldn't hurt either of them.

It was different with Katy. Her pinched face and sunken eyes, her wandering mind, told them that a stout heart had kept her going about as far as it could. Unless they got her out of the wilderness quickly she would never complete that visit to her grandfather.

Idly Hank wondered what that grandfather, whoever he might be, would be thinking now.

In the Air Service communications center Donahue muttered constantly and meaninglessly to himself. The ordeal of waiting had taken the orator's boom out of his voice and the florid color out of his cheeks. He looked old and sick and beaten, like a toothless lion.

"Forest Service," he mumbled. "Inhuman, incompetent. I'll cut the Forest Service to ribbons."

"Will that bring Katy back?" retorted Captain Donahue gloomily. "Forget it, Dad. These people have already done more than anyone else could. I think Crawford's working on some new idea now."

There was no answer. The one soft spot in the heart of the old pirate had been for his granddaughter. There was nothing left in him now but hate.

Around the big map table, Crawford was the center of a group that included Hank's father, Regional Forester Manley, Fire Chief Morrow and Dr. Small. Ben Gray, the dispatcher, pulled off his earphones and joined them.

"Message from Stemple, boss," he said. "They've

finished combing the fire area and found no—found nothing. It's certain they weren't trapped."

"And they headed south because the fires were thinnest on that side," added Crawford. "Let's go on from there. The first thing they'd come to would be the Whitetail Marsh."

Senator Winton objected, "Wouldn't they be more likely to skirt the fire, looking for a ground crew?" He was haggard and nervous too, but not as worried as his colleague. Better acquainted with the ability of foresters to look after themselves, he had more confidence.

"By themselves, yes," replied Crawford. "With the child on their hands, no. You must realize that everything those boys would do depends on the girl. Put it this way. She's a burden, a fairly heavy one, awkward to carry and very fragile. It would be like —like playing football with a goldfish bowl for a helmet. Most important of all, she can't be abandoned in an emergency, like a piece of equipment."

"That's what they probably did, though," snarled Donahue. "Tossed her aside to save themselves. And now they're skulking, afraid to show themselves."

All at once Senator Winton's iron self control

broke. In a voice low but deadly with rage he said, "One of those smokejumpers happens to be my son, Donahue. Be a little careful."

"Your son?" stammered Donahue, his face the color of putty. "I didn't know. I didn't know."

Crawford continued, "Their first move would be to put some distance between them and the fire. I place them at the marsh the first night. It would take them about that long to get there and find out that the marsh has no outlet. They'd be looking for a watercourse, naturally, to lead them out of the country, having no maps."

"Maybe they're still at Whitetail, waiting for someone to hunt them up," suggested the Fire Chief.

Crawford studied this proposal. "Maybe. But I don't think so. Especially not that pair. Smokejumpers aren't trained to sit down and wait. I see it this way. They didn't get my message not to go south. If they had they'd have doubled back and run into a party by now. I say they climbed this low mountain range south of the marsh looking for another watercourse. And that puts them into the old 1910 burn."

Crawford was making the struggle of the smoke-jumpers so plain and so realistic that even Donahue had joined the circle around the map.

"What is this thing you call a burn?" he asked. "Could they have trouble there?"

"It's a deathtrap," stated Crawford flatly. "They could only travel by walking fallen logs. One spark blown in from the other fire or from lightning and it blows up. One misstep and you're down with a broken leg. This much I'm sure of, they'd never stop until they got out of it. And if they are out, they're in tough shape. I'll make you a long guess. Assuming no accidents, I place them now somewhere around this little unnamed lake." He drew a red circle on the map around Lake Katy.

Dr. Small said, "Then the thing to do is make a jump onto this lake. Well, what are we waiting for?" The parachute doctor quivered with impatience.

Crawford shook his head. "Not so fast. We've got to allow for trouble in the burn."

"What is your plan then?" asked the Regional Forester.

"The doc and I will make our jump onto the marsh; cut the trail there. It will save time in the end. They'd have to chop through the burn and we can follow the line twice as fast as they made it."

Manley spoke sadly, plainly hating every word. "Two isn't a strong enough party. I shouldn't let you jump at all. You're not in training for it. I won't let you unless you can dig up some more help."

"You know every other jumper in the region is down on a fire," cried Crawford angrily. "It would take days to get even one out and re-equipped."

Stubbornly the Regional Forester shook his head.

Then Crawford's baffled face cleared. "I've got it. Will you go for three?"

"Yes," said Manley, "I'll go for three."

"Ben," Crawford snapped, "get Wimpfelburger in here. He's next door in the parachute loft." To the others he explained, "This man is a jumper we converted into a parachute rigger." If he was stretching the facts a little, no one was present who could challenge him.

Wimpy came trotting in with his eager smile and halted, abashed before so much brass.

"Wimpy," said Crawford, "Hank and Jim are down somewhere in the Idaho wilderness and in trouble. Will you jump with me to help them out?"

It was Joseph Wimpfelburger's great hour and he met it without hesitating a fraction of a second: "I know about it. Yes sir, I'll jump."

ONLY SOMEONE who knew them well would have recognized the members of the little party that inched doggedly through the Idaho wilderness. That ragged, sweat-stained tramp, hobbling painfully with a tree trunk as a crutch, could hardly be Jim Dade, the fastest man with his fists in the Air Service. Who would see a squad leader of smokejumpers, or the son of a senator, in the haggard giant who shuffled along, one cautious, fearful step at a time? On the giant's shoulders perched a scarecrow, surely not the little girl who had flown in brave new finery to visit her grandfather.

They had been traveling like this for hours, from the cool of the morning, through the heat of midday, into the cool of the afternoon. And it was useless. In three days their skill and determined effort had found not one sign of humanity, not a blaze on a tree nor the mark of a shod hoof nor the ashes of a campfire. They had suffered inhuman punishment; they were done for and they knew it. Yet some indomitable spark kept them going aimlessly forward.

"We're coming to another canyon," said Jim dully. "Ought to be something in it."

They plodded on until at last Jim stopped Hank by catching his elbow as the smokejumper shuffled blindly past.

"This the canyon?" asked Hank.

"Yep."

"Trail in it?"

"Nope. Unless on the other side of the creek."

"Well, better luck next canyon."

But without speaking of it, they knew that this was as far as they could go.

Jim lifted the half-conscious child from Hank's shoulders. He guided Hank to a tree where the blind smokejumper could sit with a back rest. He laid Katy carefully on the ground, and sat down himself.

"Think I'll take a sashay across the creek," croaked Jim after a while. "Absolutely ought to be a road or a trail or a telephone line in a canyon this size."

"Maybe even a telephone booth," giggled Hank.

"I'd cut a wire, dope. Bring a trouble shooter," retorted literal-minded Jim.

He tried to get up, struggling for several seconds in grim silence before he made it. He could stand as long as he held onto the tree. But the first step away from it, his one good leg buckled and threw him. He dragged himself back.

"You still there, Jim?" asked Hank, peering blindly.

"Yep."

"I've got a better idea. Take Katy with you and go."

"Nope."

"You've got to," pleaded the sightless giant. "Nothing makes sense unless——"

"You darn fool," interrupted Jim savagely. "I can't go, even if you talked me into it, even if Gabriel blew his horn. I tried."

It was then that they heard the sound. It was very close, but at first unrecognizable to their dull senses. Hank, his blind face with the dreadfully swollen eyelids turned toward it, heard it first.

Irrepressible even then, he grinned in the direction of Jim's voice and said, "He heard you. Old Gabe's tuning up his trumpet."

All through that agonizing day they had heard the plane that droned persistently overhead, above the pall of smoke. But they paid no attention. It was probably a patrol ship looking for new fires. There was no reason why it should have anything to do with them.

Yet about the time they were leaving Lake Katy, Crawford, "Little Doc" and Wimpy had tumbled out of that very plane and floated down through the blue mist into the Whitetail Marsh. The Air Service Chief had steered them deliberately into a soft, damp landing in the shallow water and thick grass. After all, not one of the three except the doctor was in real jumping condition, and they couldn't afford any injuries.

Ignoring the doctor's comments as he fished his medical kit out of the mud, Crawford began to search. Like a wolf he sniffed out the spot where Hank and Jim and Katy had camped. A few more minutes, and he was coursing along their trail over the mountain range with the doctor and Wimpy puffing behind.

Crawford in action was a sight to remember. He stalked across country on his long legs like a moose, never bothering to go round an obstruction he could crash or jump. Seldom at fault, he went from a caulk scratch on a rock to a scuff mark in the dust to an uprooted sod to a broken branch, tracing the climb of the smokejumpers up over the cliffs and down the other side of the range to the edge of the burn. There he was momentarily baffled, which gave his companions a chance to overtake him.

"Wonder if I could slip up on that guy and hobble him," remarked Dr. Small fretfully. A noted trailburner himself, he had never been led such a chase in his life.

Wimpy merely looked at him and panted like a dog. Presently Crawford made a cast into the burn, running the logs on his steel-shod feet like a great cat. Quickly he found one of Dade's axe marks and waved his party on. Where Hank and Jim had been forced to chop and inch their way along, the rescue party ran, or rather danced. They were unencumbered and had a cleared path.

At this game the doctor, active as a squirrel, was Crawford's match. Wimpy had more trouble. Twice he missed his footing on the treacherous logs and fell. But smokejumper training saved him. Each time he saved himself from injury, dragged himself up out of the tangle and kept going. In a few hours they covered the ground that had cost the fleeing smokejumpers a full day.

At Lake Katy, the doctor and Wimpy were glad to rest in the abandoned camp while Crawford puzzled out what had happened there. To his wilderness-trained senses a bit of paper, a scrap of cloth, a footprint told as complete a story as if it had been written. He prowled the woods and gave the others a running account of what he found.

"Their last meal," he said, holding up the empty meat tin. "At least one of them was hurt. Bandages have been cut out of the parachute. I found a footprint that wasn't made by a shoe. They were in bad shape when they left here. Wouldn't have discarded the parachute otherwise. It was their tent and sleeping bag."

He even found the makeshift fishing rod Jim Dade had thrown away with such disgust and read its story: "They counted on eating out of the lake. Probably meant to rest up until they were fit to travel again. Barren lake. That tore it."

After a wider circle around the camp and down the lake shore, Crawford came back and sat down. Dr. Small looked at him questioningly.

"We're close now," said Crawford. "So we've got to slow down and be careful. Easy to miss them. They aren't traveling with a plan any more. Too beat up and exhausted. They're just going. I figure it this way. Dade has hurt his foot; axe cut, maybe, or he fell in the burn. The girl's either hurt or too weak to walk. There's one footprint she made in the camp. None anywhere else."

"At least that settles one thing, they've still got her," said the doctor savagely.

"Did you ever doubt it?" queried the Air Service Chief. "Hank puzzles me. I've found a line of his tracks, and he walks unnaturally. Much too short a stride for that big galoot, and all spraddled out as if he wasn't sure of his footing, like he'd grope his way in the dark. Probably fatigue and carrying the girl."

"How about smoke blindness?" suggested the doctor, who knew quite a lot about firefighting himself.

"Of course, that's it," agreed Crawford. "Hank was smoked up last summer and got another good dose when they broke out from the plane."

For a moment he was silent and the three, each for himself, could picture the hopeless and bitter struggle that must be going on somewhere beyond the lake.

"Let's go," begged Wimpy, unable to stand his thoughts any longer.

"While you were beagling around in the brush, I was studying the map," said the doctor. "This canyon runs into another bigger one that has a road in it. Road leads to a boy scout camp. D'you suppose they have any idea how close they are to safety?"

"How could they? But a road and a scout camp. That's perfect! We'll head direct for that camp. We can make it by dark and have a gang of scouts out hunting those poor devils." Crawford unslung his parachutist's radio and made contact with the plane which hovered faithfully overhead.

"Crawford to pilot. Expect to locate our party within next two or three hours. Notify base. Have Winton, Donahue and Donahue's son flown to nearest airfield. Arrange motor transportation to take them to Boy Scout camp on Snowdrift Creek. Over."

"Roger. Willco. Pilot clear and out," came the reply, and the droning faded away.

The canyon was full of shadows as Crawford led the rescue party on the final leg of its journey. The light was too poor for trailing. They headed for the road, pausing now and then to listen and call. But they reached the road and the Scout camp without any sign of the missing group.

It took only a moment to explain the situation to the scoutmaster and his patrol leaders. In five minutes a hundred Scouts were panting to be off on the search.

Crawford said, "I think half of the group ought to spread out along the road. If Hank and Jim keep going long enough, they're bound to come to it. Divide the rest into parties of three and four and scatter them out through the woods. No telling where you'll find them."

It was tantalizing to be so near the end of the search, to know that Hank and Jim and Katy might be within a quarter-mile of the camp, down and helpless.

"I have a suggestion," put in the scoutmaster. "I'll have our bugler play calls. Maybe they'll hear, know that help is close."

"Wonderful," agreed Crawford. Even with the help of the Scouts he knew only too well how easy it would be to miss the castaways in the darkness and the immensity of the wilderness. Time would be short for them now. If they hadn't made the road, they were in the last extremity.

"Hear that bugle," Crawford pleaded silently. "Give us a signal. Start a fire, anything. Just one more punch does it."

The Scout trumpeter ran a few practice notes. Then he turned the silver throat of his instrument toward the wilderness and blew the stirring music of "To The Colors" and "Retreat."

To Hank and Jim, the sound was incredibly clear and close. Surrounded by dense forest, unable to see over a hundred feet in any direction, they could hear the invisible bugler warming his lips. There was a pause. In imagination they could hear him draw a deep breath. Then through all the tree-clad peaks and canyons the triumphant music rang.

Crawford's wolf-sharp eyes spotted them first. He saw something white bobbing along at ground level. Then the scarecrow figure of Jim Dade materialized out of the gloom, hopping on his crutch. After him shambled the giant figure of Hank holding a tiny body in his arms.

Dr. Small lunged forward at almost the same moment, but Crawford's steel fingers held him back.

"What's the idea?" growled the doctor, struggling to get free.

"They made it on their own," said the grim firefighter. "Let 'em finish it."

✿ CONCLUSION ✿

THE RECUPERATIVE powers of youth are amazing. Carried bodily into their encampment by the scouts, fussed and exclaimed over, washed, bandaged and stuffed with food, Hank, Jim and Katy were almost back to normal in a few hours.

Dr. Small quickly eased the throbbing in Jim's foot and poured a soothing lotion into Hank's inflamed eyes. Presently Hank even had a slit of vision, and the swelling went down.

During this time messengers, telephones and radios had been busy. A plane, loaded with more brass than the Forest Service bush pilot had ever seen at one time in his life, roared off the Midvale airfield. Even at that moment a motorcade was spraying clouds of dust and gravel along a narrow canyon road.

When Hank and Jim saw the first passenger to jump out, heard Katy cry "Granddaddy," and saw her run into the arms of Senator Donahue, they could think of nothing to say.

Katy came to them pulling along her grandfather, and cried, "I want you to meet Hank and Jim. They saved me."

At that moment one of the nation's most voluble orators could think of nothing to say, either.

Somewhat later Senator Winton asked him baldly, "What do you think of smokejumpers now?"

Whatever else there was to be said about Donahue, he was a good loser. "Finest collection of fighting men in the world," he stated. "You can quote me."

1822